Networks of Trust

Networks of Trust

THE SOCIAL COSTS OF COLLEGE
AND WHAT WE CAN DO ABOUT THEM

Anthony Simon Laden

The University of Chicago Press

CHICAGO AND LONDON

The University of Chicago Press, Chicago 60637
The University of Chicago Press, Ltd., London
© 2024 by The University of Chicago
Published 2024
Printed in the United States of America

33 32 31 30 29 28 27 26 25 24   1 2 3 4 5

ISBN-13: 978-0-226-83717-8 (cloth)
ISBN-13: 978-0-226-83719-2 (paper)
ISBN-13: 978-0-226-83718-5 (e-book)
DOI: https://doi.org/10.7208/chicago/9780226837185.001.0001

Library of Congress Cataloging-in-Publication Data

Names: Laden, Anthony Simon, 1967– author.
Title: Networks of trust : the social costs of college and what we can
    do about them / Anthony Simon Laden.
Description: Chicago : The University of Chicago Press, 2024. |
    Includes bibliographical references and index.
Identifiers: LCCN 2024011757 | ISBN 9780226837178 (cloth) |
    ISBN 9780226837192 (paperback) | ISBN 9780226837185 (ebook)
Subjects: LCSH: Education, Higher—Social aspects—United States. |
    Education—Aims and objectives.
Classification: LCC LA227.4 .L334 2024 | DDC 378.73—dc23/eng/20240403
LC record available at https://lccn.loc.gov/2024011757

♾ This paper meets the requirements of ANSI/NISO Z39.48-1992
(Permanence of Paper).

For Clara

Contents

{1}

Introduction

I used to teach a class called "Introduction to Ethics" that focused on racism and sexism. I only assigned readings by radical feminists and critical race theorists. I did not try to present many sides of the issues we discussed, but I also wasn't trying to convince students to adopt the viewpoint of the authors we read. I wanted to teach students to think through an unfamiliar theoretical perspective that took work to understand. One of the unheralded but valuable skills students can learn from studying philosophy is what philosophers call "charitable thinking." To approach a position or argument charitably means to take it seriously and try to understand how a smart, thoughtful, and careful person might hold a view like that; why, even if it looks at first as if it must be wrong, there are good reasons why others don't think it is.[1] I hoped to help students develop this skill through an in-depth engagement with a single theoretical point of view. For a student strongly opposed to that view, however, the class could look one-sided, perhaps even an exercise in indoctrination.

I tried to dispel this worry each semester. I insisted to my students that the class had no party line. I told them that their assignments would be graded on the clarity of their thought and expression and not the positions they took or defended. I told them that a paper criticizing the authors we read or what I said in class had as much chance to earn a good grade as one that defended them.

There were always students who were skeptical. One semester, a conservative student from a religious Christian background received a bad grade for a paper he wrote that criticized an author we had read. He asked to meet with me to discuss his grade, which he felt was the result of the position he took. We set up a time to meet, and when he arrived at my office door, he was accompanied by his father.

We began talking about the student's paper and I explained why I thought the grade was justified—not because I disagreed with its conclusions or the position the student defended, but because the writing and reasoning were unclear. The conversation eventually moved on to the course itself, and their concern that it was one-sided, biased, and unfair. I offered some of the rationales listed above for my design of the course, and pointed out that a college education could be broad-based and well-rounded even if each particular course was not. At some point, though, I shifted my perspective. Rather than defending my professional choices as a teacher, or an abstract idea of college education, I thought about the father's position as a father. I had young children at the time who were just starting school. I said that I admired his decision to send his son to a public university where he would be exposed to classes like mine and might come away with views different from those he had been raised with. I said it was a really brave thing to do and that as a parent, I wasn't sure I would have that courage. I thanked him for his willingness to do that and the trust that involved.

That changed the tenor of the conversation. It became less oppositional. It felt like we could all let our guard down. The father said he wasn't worried about his son's values or religious beliefs being transformed by his time in college. He was confident in his son's upbringing. I assured him that I wasn't trying to change those beliefs, just trying to help his son learn to think well about complex issues and not merely dismiss views he disagreed with. By the time they left my office, I don't think I had really convinced either of them of the content of what I had said, but it did seem as if I had begun to earn their trust.

For years I looked back on that exchange as a relative success. I had a defensible and clearly articulated rationale for what and how I taught. At the same time, I was sufficiently appreciative of the anxieties it provoked that I could calm them by being genuinely grateful for the trust placed in me. In the end, the students who came into the class disagreeing with me weren't really worried that I would convert them to a position they rejected. As long as I wasn't grading them on their conformity to a party line, I wasn't doing anything that was wrong or that required more care than I was giving it.

Now, years later, I am not so sure. Not about teaching a class with the focus that one had, but about the source of the worries that brought that student and his father to my door, and what a fully adequate response to those worries would have required. While shifting to the terrain of trust was a move in the right direction, I failed to appreciate fully the source of their concern. I expressed my gratitude that a father would entrust me with his child, and in particular with the formation of his child's beliefs. It turned out that he wasn't worried about that, because he didn't think his son's beliefs were in danger of being changed by anything I did. He was probably right about that.

What I did not then understand and so failed to address was that I, and the university as a whole, were engaged in a very different process: one that would, if successful, change his son in more fundamental ways. We were reshaping who and what he trusted.

* * *

This book grows from that thought. It places trust and the building of trust, rather than beliefs, values, and their formation, at the center of its picture of education. It explores that new picture and what it reveals. It suggests that we pay more attention to the role formal education plays in shaping what I call students' "informational trust networks." These are the complex networks of people and institutions a person trusts when she takes up what they produce and transmit as information with which to think. Building trust networks is neither an explicit aim of those who teach nor, so understood, the way most people—including teachers—think teaching works. As with informational trust networks themselves, the shaping of those networks happens in the background, and so is easy to overlook.

Because education shapes how students build their informational trust networks, it affects who and what they trust. Our informational trust networks, even more than our beliefs and values, shape and are shaped by our social networks. We can converse and engage with people even when we don't share their beliefs and values. When other people do not share our informational trust networks, however, it is difficult to have the sorts of easy conversations that build and maintain intimacy and familiarity. A focus on trust thus illuminates one way education affects and possibly harms students, their families, and their communities. When the process of education results in students inhabiting informational trust networks very different from those in which they grew up, the very process of becoming educated places stress on at least some of their social ties. For many students, as well as their families and communities, that stress imposes a considerable cost.

In a diverse, modern society, members of different communities often do not occupy the same or even similar or overlapping trust networks. This makes the task educational institutions face more difficult and more fraught. If, in a given society, being educated involves coming to occupy the trust networks associated with one particular group of people, then the costs and burdens of education will fall unequally across the society: some people will emerge from their education with trust networks that resemble those of the people around whom they grew up and some will not. Once we see our education system as functioning this way, we can better appreciate why certain communities are anxious about its effects—not only the sort of conservative religious community to which my student and his father belonged, but also poor and minoritized as well as rural and traditional communities. Schools and colleges that build informational trust networks for students that are fundamentally different from the networks people in their communities inhabit do more or less what some people in those communities fear. Easing their anxiety will require that schools and colleges discharge the task of building trust networks responsibly, with proper care and concern for those they affect: both their students and those back home. In short, it will require that schools and colleges be trustworthy.

There is a further reason to take seriously this duty of trustworthiness. Even if the trust networks educational institutions build for their students are better tools for understanding the world than those the students leave behind, schools and colleges that move students from a variety of trust networks into one inhabited by a particular segment of the population will ultimately play an anti-democratic role. In a democratic society, citizens have to work out together how they will live together. Democratic societies can only sustain their democratic character if their members can talk productively with one another. Such talk requires that people do not inhabit completely unconnected trust networks; it requires that society is not made up of a set of distinct cognitive islands. Two people whose informational trust networks don't overlap at all (who inhabit different cognitive islands) will tend to find each other inscrutable. Each one thinks with a completely different set of ingredients and relies on different criteria in determining which ingredients to use. Even if they accept that they must live together, they won't be able to work out together how to do so.

If education merely moves some students off the cognitive islands where they grew up and resettles them onto another one rather than helping people who occupy distinct informational trust networks talk more easily to one another, it will undermine rather than aid the democratic project. Occupants of the islands from which children are removed will not merely see those on the island to which their children are resettled as different from them and inscrutable; they will come to see college teachers and perhaps college-educated people generally as predators or oppressors. Rather than accept the judgments of college-credentialed experts about how to organize the common society, these parents and communities will resist and resent their pronouncements. In many cases, they will be right to do so.

The question of how educational institutions work and the effects they have on their students thus has importance beyond the classroom. The building of trust in education—both in the sense of how education builds student trust networks and in whether or not educational institutions are worthy of our trust as they do that—is thus a project that concerns us all.

*   *   *

There are several steps along the path to this conclusion that need filling in. Chapter 2 introduces a general characterization of trust as the acceptance of vulnerability. This clarifies what makes something worthy of trust and explains why anxiety is a natural response to the lack of trustworthiness. It develops the idea of an informational trust network, as well as two other forms of trust that play a key role in education. It thus explains the central role trust plays both in education itself and within the institutions we task with educating children and young adults. Chapter 3 argues that formal education, especially at the college level, shapes students' informational trust networks. It argues that many colleges build what I describe as a broadly scientific trust network for their students, and describes that network's key features. Chapter 4 then examines the effects of transforming students' trust networks. It argues that a college education which aims to build one particular trust network might impose costs on students who arrive on campus inhabiting a variety of different trust networks. It suggests that debates about whether colleges are indoctrinating their students or whether they are sufficiently inclusive and welcoming can be better understood through this lens. This completes the diagnosis outlined above. The final two chapters suggest strategies colleges and universities could use to be more trustworthy. Chapter 5 analyzes some pedagogical projects that might improve the trustworthiness of students' trust networks. It describes an informational trust network that, if built by educational institutions, would shift the social costs of being educated and produce citizens capable of bridging the gaps between cognitive islands rather than merely relocating students from one island to another. It suggests educational aims and strategies that would foster the building of such a network. Chapter 6 looks at further steps colleges and universities could take to build their students' trust in higher education.

* * *

While this book addresses itself to a wider audience, it is a book of philosophy, by a philosopher. These facts shape the nature of its argument, its scope, and its limits. This book is an exercise in what I like to call "conceptual optometry." Conceptual optometrists develop, refine, and compare sets of conceptual lenses that help us to see and think about the world in various ways. By using the concepts developed, readers may notice features of the world that were otherwise hidden or obscured or see things that were always in plain sight with a different kind of focus. Like any set of lenses, these lenses also obscure and distort aspects of our vision or the phenomena we examine with them even as they clarify and bring into focus other aspects. Their value lies not in giving us a complete and true vision of the world, but in being helpful as we try to make sense of things we care about.

A set of lenses aids, but does not substitute for, the work of looking carefully at the world. I try to show the potential value of the lenses being constructed here by describing what particular features of education and society look like when we use them. To do that, I rely on a mix of empirical research, what I take to be common and warranted understandings of certain phenomena, and my own experience as a student, parent, and teacher: someone who has spent his whole life in and around educational institutions. In doing so, I invite you to see if this is how the world of education looks to you once you use the lenses constructed in the following pages. No doubt, in some cases you will think it doesn't: that I am either misinformed about what is happening in education or am only describing a local patch of the vast field educational institutions comprise. In those cases, I ask you not to dismiss the work of the book immediately. The eye chart in your optometrist's office is far from an accurate picture of the world outside that you want to see clearly with your new glasses. But to criticize it on those grounds would be to mistake its function. Similarly, rather than rejecting the lens because of the mistakes in the eye chart, treat the concrete descriptions as illustrations designed to bring out the features of the lenses rather than as empirical claims about the world we see through them. Ask yourself if the examples help you use the lenses on offer and then whether the lenses themselves are helpful for you as you try to see clearly whatever part of higher education concerns you.

The conceptual aims of the book also shape where it focuses its attention: the eye chart it uses to show off the lenses it crafts. Much of what I have to say about trust and its place in education—about the shaping of informational trust networks and the social costs the very process of education can impose—applies to all forms of education, from pre-K all the way up to postgraduate studies. The book focuses, however, almost entirely on higher education at the undergraduate level. There are several reasons for this: Even if earlier stages of education have a more profound effect on students, the possibility that education puts stresses on social ties increases the further up the educational ladder you go. As education progresses from elementary to secondary school to college and beyond, institutions get bigger, they draw their students from a wider pool, and they teach a smaller percentage of the population. As they get older, and their school becomes more demanding, students also spend less time under the direct guidance of family members. All these factors mean that someone is more likely to emerge from college than from middle school with an informational trust network at odds with that of her family or her community. Higher education is also the educational space I know best and thus am most competent to comment on. I hope that the tools developed here will also be helpful in thinking through issues in elementary and secondary education, but to what extent they are is left as an exercise for the reader.

Of course, higher education is not a single space. There is a vast difference between private four-year residential colleges that reject the vast majority of their applicants and community colleges that offer a range of two-year degrees, only some of which are meant to feed into BA programs, where students commute from home and no one is turned away. The diversity of programs, the range of funding levels, the distribution of costs, and the variety of outcomes is all much wider in the spaces of higher education than in K-12 education. The examples offered here will of necessity not be representative of all these spaces simultaneously. I have tried to avoid the common mistake made by many commentators on higher education of focusing my attention on the most elite sectors and assuming they are representative. But I am surely blinkered in my appreciation of the full diversity of the field in view. That alone shouldn't mean the conceptual lenses on offer here are similarly limited in their value, but they may turn out to reveal different phenomena when used to examine educational spaces I have overlooked.

Some readers will no doubt resist the suggestions in the book that higher education imposes costs in ways that harm some students and their communities even as they educate them. They will insist that the process of education is, at least if done well and properly, an unalloyed good and that those who would criticize it are confused and, perhaps unknowingly, aiding malevolent social forces. They will be concerned that I am giving too much credence to the concerns expressed by bad-faith political actors or those with an agenda designed to destroy what they hold good. They will worry that in my perhaps laudable attempts to be self-critical and open-minded, I am unwittingly aiding the work of dark forces in our society. No doubt, some of these readers will think I am giving too much credence to voices on the right who raise complaints about the attempts by left-wing faculty to indoctrinate their students. Others will think I am giving too much credence to voices on the left who claim that colleges are insufficiently inclusive, both as social spaces and in the orientation of their curriculum. Many of these readers will work in education and I would venture that all of them will be the products of higher education. If you are such a reader, I would ask you to try to see the institutions and spaces you (and I) value and contribute to not as familiar but as alien and vaguely threatening, and to take seriously the thought that for all the wondrous good these institutions do and can do, they may also do a fair amount of harm, and that the two may be more intertwined than we like to admit.

Those harms are not hard to find once you begin to look for them. Start with the fact that the six-year graduation rate from all US colleges in 2022 was 62.3 percent.[2] That means that more than a third of those who started college in the US in 2016 did not finish it by 2022: an impersonal statistic that covers a variety of social and institutional obstacles, as well as human suffering and trauma. Then move on to students like Todd, a Black foreign service officer with a master's degree from an Ivy League university, who grew up in a high poverty, high crime, but close-knit neighborhood of Atlanta, transferred out of his local public school to a mostly white magnet school, and then went away to college. Each step on this educational journey pulled him further away from, and made it harder for him to maintain relationships with, those back home. Todd describes his experience of college like this: "It was almost like I was given the choice . . . to sacrifice relationships for being able to survive college."[3] Continue on to Robin Wall Kimmerer, a young Potawatomi woman meeting her college advisor for the first time and explaining that she wanted to study botany to understand why asters and goldenrod looked so beautiful together:

"Miss Wall," he said, fixing me with a disappointed smile, "I must tell you that *that* is not science. That is not at all the sort of thing with which botanists concern themselves." But he promised to put me right. . . . I had no rejoinder; I had made a mistake. There was no fight in me, only embarrassment at my error. I did not have words for resistance. . . . I didn't think about it at the time, but it was happening all over again, an echo of my grandfather's first day at school, when he was ordered to leave everything—language, culture, family—behind. The professor made me doubt where I came from, what I knew, and claimed that his was the *right* way to think. Only he didn't cut my hair off.[4]

Finally, come back to my student's father, who was, I think, not there merely to help his son improve his grade, but because of a deeper (if vaguer) sense that this large and rather opaque institution where his son studied might be doing something neither of them had bargained for when he enrolled. I hope that by attending to these stories and the realities they point to, you will remain open to the following thought: for institutions of higher education to be worthy of the trust necessary to do the wondrous good of which they are capable, they (we) need to be more attentive and responsive to, and less defensive about, the harms they (we) currently do along the way. This book represents my attempt to do so.

{2}

Trust in Education

In order to think about trust, in education or anywhere else, it helps to start with vulnerability. A person is vulnerable when she is subject to change by external forces that are not fully under her control. Being vulnerable is generally uncomfortable and sometimes even dangerous. It is a breeding ground for anxiety. So it is not surprising that people who are vulnerable often try to eliminate their vulnerability. They lock their doors and raise their shields. They strive to surveil and control the actions and actors to which they are vulnerable.

Though it is usual to think of vulnerability as a negative condition—as susceptibility to loss or harm—it is not always so. Outside forces can change us for the better. Being vulnerable allows us to learn new things, fall in love, or be transformed by a beautiful sunset or piece of music. Recognizing this positive side of vulnerability doesn't deny its dangers. Once we are open to change in this way, we don't get to determine which way that change will go. Being open to love requires risking heartbreak. The capacity and willingness to be awestruck by beauty requires risking being assaulted by ugliness. Nevertheless, if some forms of vulnerability have a positive side, then there is a definite cost to reducing anxiety by trying to eliminate the vulnerability that provokes it. In some cases, we may be better off finding ways to make that vulnerability acceptable.

A context or situation in which it is reasonable to accept our vulnerability is safe. It is one where, though we are vulnerable, no one and nothing is going to exploit that vulnerability to cause us harm, and where we can count on restorative care should harm befall us nevertheless. Safety, unlike security, is created not by individuals protecting themselves, but by the arrangement of the social environment more generally. I might increase my home's security by adding locks and fancy alarm systems, turning my home into a fortress with the guards always on call. But whether my neighborhood is safe or not is a function of my neighbors and their behavior rather than the number of locks on my door. It depends on their not taking advantage of each other's vulnerabilities and looking out for one another. People living in a safe neighborhood can leave their doors unlocked, take a walk at night, or let their children play outside without fear. Doing those things leaves them vulnerable to theft, assault, and loss, but the safety of the neighborhood makes it reasonable for them to accept that vulnerability.

When we trust someone or something, we make ourselves vulnerable and accept that vulnerability. Trust can thus grow from the perception that someone or something is safe. In general trust arises not from conscious choice or will, but as a response to facts and cues in our environment. Trust can, of course, be misplaced: we can be mistaken in our perception of a situation as safe or not. People trust where they should not, and fail to trust where they should. But for the most part, when trust is valuable or required and yet lacking, this is a sign that we need to change the world, not our perception of it. It suggests that we need to make spaces and activities safer, and those we encounter in those spaces need to become more trustworthy.

Because learning from others involves being changed by them, the very process of education requires and creates vulnerability. Both students and those who care about them sometimes fear what they will be taught and its effects on their lives, other beliefs, or connections. Some also worry that once they are in a vulnerable position, their teachers will exploit that vulnerability to do something other than teach them. Some parents and communities try to eliminate or contain this vulnerability by pursuing security: by trying to tightly control what is taught in classrooms and closely monitoring those doing the teaching. At the extreme, they ban books, lessons, and ideologies and surveil teachers and the institutions they work for. Since education requires vulnerability, these responses make real education difficult, if not impossible. They rob those they aim to help of the possibilities education opens up. Insofar as educational institutions encourage such responses because they are not safe or trustworthy, they fail their students.

The pursuit of safety in educational settings has a bad reputation these days. It is often thought to lead to an overzealous policing of language and behavior and the excessive coddling of young people. But it doesn't have to be this way. Thinking about safety can, rather, shine a light on the role of vulnerability in educational settings, and the possibilities of trust and trustworthiness as better responses to that vulnerability. If some parents' and students' acute awareness of their vulnerable position makes them anxious, colleges can calm that anxiety by making campuses and classrooms safe. Safety of this sort requires not adding alarms and police, or requiring full transparency and the surveillance that would make that possible, but trustworthiness. A trustworthy college would have to reduce the likelihood of harm to those students and parents, and care for them when they do suffer harms and bear costs for which they had not bargained. It could thus calm the anxiety of those who are prone to distrust college generally, while also protecting those who are liable to trust when they shouldn't.[1]

In order to be trustworthy, a college must not only care for its students generally; it must do so in ways that make clear that the school and those who work there are attuned to the particular vulnerabilities their students face. Students whose economic precarity makes it hard for them to devote sufficient time and attention to schoolwork are vulnerable in a different way than religious students who sign up for a philosophy class where morality is treated as wholly separate from religious authority. Conservative white students who take a class in US history that makes plain to them the ways race and racism have shaped US society are vulnerable in a different way than Black students who are assigned to live in a dorm or take classes in a building named after someone noted for anti-Black views or defenses of slavery, or who take a political science class in American government that portrays the US solely as a land of equality and opportunity that is open and welcoming to all. What is required to care for each student will be different, although some of the techniques for doing so may be the same. Note that making a space safe for these students does not require shielding them from any and all challenges to their views. It requires being attuned to the vulnerabilities they are being asked to accept in order to be in that space, and then thinking about whether there is a way to make those particular vulnerabilities acceptable to those students. Environments can be safe without being coddling. People can be trustworthy and yet challenge what others do, say, and think. Indeed, that is what high-quality learning looks like.

Because education and educational institutions both create and require vulnerability, educators have an obligation to be trustworthy. Since education involves a variety of forms of vulnerability, it requires trustworthiness of several different sorts:

1. Thinking, making decisions, and understanding something all require that we make use of information in direct ways. Thinking anything but the most basic thoughts requires using whole networks of information production and verification that operate in the background of the particular stretch of thinking we are doing now. Thinking is thus influenced by and so vulnerable to the information sources it relies on. How and what we think, then, is a function of which information networks we trust. Our ability to think well falters when those sources of information are mistaken, fraudulent, or otherwise unreliable. The central claim of this book is that education builds and rebuilds these "informational trust networks" as it aims to improve students' abilities. This process, even though it unfolds in the background, needs to be trustworthy.

2. When we engage in joint projects and collective actions, our collaborators and colleagues can enhance our individual actions, but they can also frustrate or corrupt them. Accepting this vulnerability requires a form of social trust in our colleagues and co-participants, and so we have reason to demand that they be trustworthy. Education is a collective activity in two important senses. First, the activity of teaching requires the effective cooperation of students and teachers. Second, educational institutions require all sorts of further collaborative activities—among teachers, between teachers and administrators, and between both these groups and students, parents, and the wider public. Education thus requires social trust, so educators need to be socially trustworthy.

3. When students enroll in a class or a college, they entrust someone with their care. They become vulnerable to various harms, and

those who love them become vulnerable to loss. Teachers and the educational institutions they work in thus have a responsibility to be trustworthy caretakers, so that those who entrust them with such care can reasonably accept the vulnerability this demands.

Each of these forms of vulnerability and trust—informational trust, social trust, and the entrusting of care—raise issues in educational contexts that help frame controversies and debates. Before looking at each of them in more detail, note that the activity of teaching combines all three, so the trustworthiness required of teachers will be multidimensional. Good and responsible teachers engage simultaneously in three sorts of activities: they care for their students, they work with their students, and they train their students to engage with new sorts of information in new ways. Teachers can fail along any of these dimensions while nevertheless doing the others well. The college professor who is an expert in her field, and an expert pedagogue, but does not show care and concern for the effect of her teaching on her students or the effects of other aspects of their lives on their ability to learn in her classroom is trustworthy along the first two dimensions, but not in the third. The kindly and concerned lecturer who never learned how to teach effectively knows what sorts of information in his field of expertise to trust, and shows concern for his students, but fails to be a trustworthy collaborator in the joint activity of passing on his knowledge. He fails at the second while succeeding at the first and third. Finally, a teacher who is well trained in the arts of pedagogy and cares for her students, but whose knowledge of the field is outdated or unreliable, will fail to initiate her students into trustworthy information networks even if she is an otherwise trustworthy presence in the classroom. Among the many reasons that teaching well is hard, and those who succeed at it a marvel, is that it requires all three sorts of trustworthiness. Seeing the differences among them can help diagnose where and when teachers fall short (if they do) and help identify more precisely the remedies needed to help them do better.

Informational Trust Networks and the Shape of Knowledge

I have to meet a friend for lunch and also run an errand. I stop to consider whether I have time to run the errand first, and check my watch to see what time it is. In the normal course of things, I look at my watch and calculate my timing based on it. I don't stop to wonder if my watch might have stopped thirty minutes ago or started running fast all of a sudden. I assume that my watch is accurate and that the time is as shown on its face. I use the information it provides to figure out if I can squeeze in my errand before lunch. Thinking, even in this mundane case, often requires outsourcing—in this case, the outsourcing of information about the accurate time to my watch. This outsourcing, however, leaves us vulnerable to misinformation and manipulation. My planning will go wrong if it turns out that my watch has failed me.

For better or worse, such vulnerability is endemic to the condition of a thinking being. In order to think about something, I have to think *with* other bits of information, and I can't think *about* those bits of information as I am thinking *with* them. There is always some amount of unquestioning acceptance going on. (I can, of course, shift my attention to the information I am thinking with and think about it—I can wonder if my watch is accurate—but doing so changes what I am thinking about and so doesn't resolve the issue.) Moreover, even if we could think both about and with some information simultaneously, a lot of our thinking requires using information we can only accept as correct, because we lack the knowledge and expertise to confirm its accuracy independently.[2]

Attempts to eliminate this vulnerability by being hypervigilant or skeptical will come up short at some point. We could learn to tell time by reference to the position of the sun or stars (when we are outside), or arrange for some official timekeeper to check in on our watch every couple of minutes, but even then we will be relying on the accuracy of our senses and memory (about how to translate visual cues into information about the time) or on the accuracy of the official timekeeper. Since there is no way to exhaustively verify all the information we rely on, and because moving any considerable distance along that path has very real costs, we need to look for safety rather than security. We need to trust, and find conditions where such trust is well placed.

The trust we need here takes the form of what the philosopher C. Thi Nguyen calls "an unquestioning attitude."[3] In the example above, I don't merely rely on my watch to tell me the right time. I trust it. I accept what it tells me without questioning it, at least in the moment. In a similar way, I trust my memory to accurately represent my past thoughts and experiences, the ground I walk on not to give way beneath my feet, my phone's mapping app to guide me accurately through an unfamiliar city, and my search engine to direct me accurately toward information on the internet without an ulterior motive or purpose. Nguyen argues that in all these cases we are trusting, and not merely relying. As he describes it, "To trust something is to *let it in*, to let it muck about directly with one's practical and cognitive innards. To trust something is to attempt to bring it *inside* of one's practical functioning."[4] Our trust in sources of information is better grounded in some cases than in others. Having to trust a source of information does not make it trustworthy.

Trusting some sources of information, however, is necessary for finite and limited creatures like us. Just as we need tools and colleagues to achieve our ends, we need information we ourselves have not fully vetted in order to think.[5] This kind of trust plays a role not only when we input simple information like the time directly into our thought processes, but when we treat all sorts of information as settled fact in order to think with it. Reading the newspaper one morning, I read that the unemployment rate is high and going up. Sitting down to do some physics homework, I read that the speed of light is constant. I take this information up as an input for further thinking. But what do I think licenses me to do that? In each case, I don't take that piece of information in isolation. If I take an unquestioning attitude about the unemployment figure, it is because I implicitly trust my daily paper. In other words, I take an unquestioning attitude about at least most of what I read in it. I don't trust what it reports because I know its reporters personally or have other sources for the same information. I trust its reporting because I implicitly extend my trust back to the processes it uses for gathering and vetting information. These include how it hires reporters and fact-checkers and its editorial process. The newspaper likely includes a sentence like "On Monday, the Bureau of Labor Statistics reported that the unemployment rate for the last month was. . . ." The reporter doesn't merely assert the information or write that it seems to her that this is the case. So part of my willingness to upload this information directly into my thinking is that I trust this source as well. Once again, in trusting the bureau's findings,

I implicitly trust that the bureau hires qualified economists and that the universities that train the economists do so well. I also have to trust that the economic and statistical theories that allow the bureau to generate a single figure from a mess of data aren't corrupt or ineffectual. My trust in both the paper and the bureau may also rest on trust in further systems that provide checks against inaccuracy and corruption. I am more willing to accept what these sources say because I trust that if they started providing false or misleading information, other agencies and institutions would notice, publicize the fact, and force them to change. I may not even realize that I am trusting all of these institutions when I accept the unemployment number. Much of our trusting happens offline, as it were, in the deep background of our thinking. But we can see the role trust plays if we imagine what happens if I don't trust some or all of these nodes. If I think my paper has ulterior motives or the bureau is massaging the data to benefit one political party or the other, then I don't unquestioningly accept the figure when I read it in my morning paper. I don't give it direct access to my thinking.

Many of our disagreements about what the facts are or whether this or that is indeed a fact are the result of our inhabiting different informational trust networks. When people say that they "believe in facts" or "believe in science," what they actually mean is that they trust a certain set of institutions and procedures, that these are part of the informational trust networks they inhabit and from which they accept information. When others are skeptical of scientific findings they are exhorted to believe or claim to believe in "alternative facts," this is often a result of not trusting those same institutions and procedures. Thinking about knowledge and claims to knowledge in terms of informational trust networks does not imply or assume that facts are subjective or that we are entitled to our own version of the facts. It is rather a recognition of how we function in a world as humans who both can and need to outsource some of our cognitive work. It suggests that some of our most heated and seemingly intractable disagreements are likely to involve disagreements about who and what to trust.

We effortlessly take up pieces of information by inhabiting large and complex networks of trust of the sort that supports my trust in my local paper's report about the unemployment rate. Inhabiting such "informational trust networks" and trusting them is not a bug in our cognitive functioning, a failure of our training, or a sign of laziness. It is what any finite creature with limited cognitive processing capacity must do. Note that the connection between our uptake of information and the informational trust networks we inhabit is relevant to practically all of the knowledge we hope to acquire in a classroom, and especially a college classroom. My knowledge of US history, theoretical physics, or even the latest management techniques comes from reading books and attending lectures. Most of what is in those books and lectures relies on other, perhaps more specialized sources that also rely on additional sources. Further knowledge mediates even conclusions drawn from basic archival and experimental evidence. Experiments often rely on machinery whose workings the scientist may not understand or question, or on other experimental work that regards this as evidence for that. Treating an archival document as evidence involves trusting processes of authentication and continuity of storage. Similar networks stand behind the more practical knowledge a student acquires in a clinical program in the health sciences or on the way to a degree in business. Trust linking these chains of support makes information at their ends usable. Because I trust my sources of information, who trust their sources of information, and so on, I treat their findings as information. That is, I allow these findings to directly inform my further thinking: I use them to think with.

This need to trust is also not a condition we tolerate as novices but then outgrow. Those doing advanced research or with long-standing experience and expertise in a particular domain also need to trust various sources of information to think about matters in those areas. Scientific and other academic research is now, of necessity, hyper-specialized and interdependent.[6] Experimental scientists rely on equipment they don't have the expertise to build. They rely on techniques that have been validated by others, and which they may not be in a position to fully evaluate. Social scientists rely on statistical tools and survey instruments which were not only developed and built and tested by others, but which they could not develop and test on their own. Doctors and other clinicians rely on studies they could not design or run, and instruments they could neither build nor properly evaluate. We all rely on processes of knowledge storage and retrieval and the processing of information by algorithms we not only don't know but probably couldn't understand. Rampant levels of informational trust run all through the higher reaches of knowledge production, transmission, and use, which creates both risks and rewards. Such trust levels allow for the sorts of collaboration that push the boundaries of our knowledge of particle physics, but they can also lead to forms of groupthink that can prevent even large numbers of smart, thoughtful, and well-intentioned people from achieving laudable goals.

For an example of the risks, consider the widespread adoption of and persistent convictions about the efficacy of so-called "whole language" methods of teaching reading in US schools. Despite persistent evidence that these methods do not actually teach children to read, including a consensus among scientists studying the cognitive processes associated with reading, many dedicated teachers, administrators, and policymakers continue to adopt and promote whole language instruction methods because they trust a mix of information sources that champion such programs. These include high-profile professors at prestigious schools of education, well-regarded publishers, and their own well-developed sense of what a classroom conducive to learning should look like. Here, a bunch of people involved in teaching reading to children inhabited similar informational trust networks that turned out not to be trustworthy.[7] As this example suggests, reliance on untrustworthy informational networks is not solely a mistake of the un- or under-educated. There is no foolproof way to have the success of collaborative work in particle physics and completely avoid cases like the adoption of flawed methods of teaching reading. The path forward is not to do away with trust or to make it completely risk-free, but to find ways of figuring out whether and where an informational trust network is trustworthy or not.

For teachers, the work of determining whether a trust network is trustworthy and convincing students and others that it is faces a further complication. Not only don't we all inhabit the same or even similar trust networks; we do not even share a sense of what makes a given informational network trustworthy. Our individual networks include various combinations of things like government agencies, scientific bodies, university-credentialed expertise, social media, neighbors, family members, and religious authorities. The nodes that make up a given person's informational trust network may be as much a result of where and with whom she grew up as they are a process of careful reflection and evaluation. This is as true for the children of college-educated professionals who tend to trust the sorts of networks colleges help to build as it is for first-generation students who grew up in tight-knit immigrant or rural or religious communities where skepticism about the knowledge produced in elite spaces and far-off institutions is more commonplace.

Though people grow up inhabiting a variety of informational trust networks, not all networks provide equally good tools for thinking. Some trust networks are better than others at delivering accurate beliefs: they are more reliable and less prone to systemic failure or error. Part of becoming better at knowing about the world is learning how to assess the trustworthiness of various trust networks and to move from those that are less trustworthy to those that are more so. This is not, however, a process we can undertake from outside our various trust networks. We can't take up a position outside of any and all networks and use that to see who is relying on "facts." And we can't just rely on the track record of university-credentialed expertise, since it is far from spotless.

How, then, should we sift through our informational trust networks to determine which is more trustworthy? It turns out that even here we disagree. For most people, their informational trust network is not merely a collection of trusted sources of information assembled more or less at random or as a result of passively adding new nodes when they are offered. Most people have at least a rough and ready set of criteria for judging whether a given source of information is trustworthy, and these criteria point to the cues they look to in order to establish trustworthiness. Often, people attend to the form in which information is presented. Information can be presented using generic language that has wide or universal reach, or it can be presented encased in situated and hyper-local terms. One source cites various figures about the rate and duration of unemployment among different groups in a neighborhood, and correlates that to various other measures of wealth, health, and well-being. Another source relates a piece of situated gossip about the fate of a particular individual who struggled with finding work and the various consequences for him of that struggle. Each passes on information about the economic state of a neighborhood, but they present that information in different forms. Those forms then point to a second kind of difference: a difference in the grounds or methods the source uses to discover the information it presents. The source that cites unemployment rates and other economic data relies on a set of methods that are used to calculate such figures: statistical sampling and economic theory as well as a categorization of employment by general types. It implicitly presents its information as trustworthy in light of its being grounded in such methods. The source that relays a piece of situated gossip relies on a different kind of method: one that values the development of situated knowledge and understanding on the basis of long acquaintance with and participation in various social practices. It also presents its information as trustworthy in light of its methods.

The set of criteria someone in an informational trust network relies on to evaluate sources creates an "informational ideology." It gives the inhabitants of a given trust network a more or less coherent story about why some sources of information fall within their network and others don't. A trust network's informational ideology sets out a view about which kinds of methods and forms of report are trustworthy. If I "believe in science," I trust the methods regarded as scientific: the ones that rely on standardization, universal claims, and generic forms to develop theories of broad reach. When someone offers me information that has this form, I am likely to trust it at least in part on the grounds that it was ascertained with the methods I trust. Someone else might be suspicious of such methods. Perhaps she is more keenly aware of the way they misdescribe or ignore local variation and detail, or she is just generally suspicious that outsiders could know more about her local situation than those with whom she shares that situation. When a person or source delivers information to her that is in scientific form and relies on scientific methods, she is likely to distrust that information and that source precisely because it is scientific.

When our different informational trust networks contain distinct and conflicting informational ideologies, our disputes about which sources of information to trust can become particularly intractable. This deep divergence among our various informational trust networks highlights another feature of our reliance on such networks that will be important as the argument of the book unfolds. People who disagree not only about what sources of information can be trusted but also about what makes a source of information trustworthy in the first place are likely to find each other inscrutable. Each will have trouble understanding how the world looks to the other or what it is like to inhabit the world in the way she does. Each may think of the other as deluded or naïve or just foolish, and thus not someone whose point of view or thoughts need to be taken seriously.

One consequence of that mutual inscrutability is that it blocks or inhibits the sorts of easy conversation that build and maintain intimacy and friendship. The sort of casual conversation I have in mind relies on a certain level of attunement between people, and one of its consequences and points is to establish and maintain such attunement. Note that the difficulty here will not be merely a result of having divergent beliefs, tastes, and values. People who disagree about beliefs, tastes, and values can have easy and casual conversations with each other. They can even have such a conversation in which they argue about those beliefs, tastes, and values. Intimacy and friendship and other close social ties can survive and even thrive in the face of such disagreements. But these ties will begin to break down when our informational trust networks completely diverge, and especially when they rest on incompatible informational ideologies. This means that the shape of our informational trust networks affects the shape of our social networks. Students whose informational trust networks undergo radical transformation in college are likely to find their social networks transformed as well. They may find their ties to their families and home communities strained and possibly broken. (This is the concern that my conversation with the religious student and his father failed to explore or address, but it is in different ways the concern of Todd, who sacrificed his relations to survive in college.) As I will argue over the next couple of chapters, one way higher education alienates some students from their families and communities involves teaching them to rely on a new kind of informational ideology as it helps them build a new informational trust network.

The connection between informational and social networks goes both ways. The easy and casual conversations we have with those in our social networks attunes us to them. That process reinforces our trust in the information they rely on and so draws the informational trust networks we inhabit closer together. This process isn't a result of mistaking our close friends and families for experts; rather, it comes from the development of a shared worldview as a result of the conversations that attune us. Moreover, it can be reinforced by the social role our informational trust networks play. If abandoning a particular informational trust network will impose social costs on me, I have reason not to do it regardless of whether it is a trustworthy path to genuine knowledge. Nor is acting on those reasons a soft-headed failure to prioritize truth over friendship. Thinking about and navigating through the world is as much a social process as an intellectual one.

Informational trust plays an important role in the very essence of higher education. Education is not the process by which we go from having to trust others to being able to think for and by ourselves. The skills of critical thinking do not free us of the need to inhabit informational trust networks; rather, they change the shape of the informational trust networks we inhabit. As I will argue in chapter 3, one of the deep effects of higher education generally is to build and refurbish students' informational trust networks. From this perspective, we can see debates about indoctrination in a different light. If I occupy a given informational trust network, then helping others to inhabit it and see it as a trustworthy source of information will look to me like education. But for those who occupy another network, the very same process will look different, especially if its target is someone they love and with whom they previously shared such a network. From their perspective, the student changes in ways that are hard to make sense of: she begins to trust people and institutions they do not and stops trusting sources they do. In other contexts, those are warning signs of an abusive relationship. It is thus easy for them to conclude that the only way such a process could be successful is that it employs methods that work around the rational, critical faculties of the student herself. In other words, those on the outside will conclude that what is happening must be the result of indoctrination, not education. The first step colleges need to take in order to be trustworthy guides in this process is to make sure the informational trust networks they help their students to inhabit are trustworthy to the highest degree possible. As a result of the close connections between social networks and informational trust networks, however, these worries are likely to persist, even if those concerned can be convinced that the new informational trust networks are themselves trustworthy. That is, the worries won't vanish even if the people, institutions, and systems they worry about have truth on their side. Since part of the source of the anxiety here does not depend on holding that students are being led to false beliefs or morally suspect values, a college can't demonstrate that it is a trustworthy caretaker of its students merely by making sure that what it teaches them is trustworthy. It must also be attentive to the costs its care may impose.

Such attention is not merely a duty of care. Colleges will have a harder time building new trust networks for students if those social costs are not factored in. Learning what a college has to teach, even if what it teaches is trustworthy, will not seem like a safe activity for students whose social networks share a very different informational trust network. They risk harm and so will want assurance that if they are, in fact, harmed, they will be cared for. Since colleges can only educate students who trust them, they have a further obligation not only to aim at trustworthy goals, but to undertake that work in a trustworthy manner. This, then, points to the need to consider the other two forms of trust implicated in the process of education.

Social Trust and Collective Action

When I engage with others in some activity, my efforts can be thwarted by what they do. If others fail to do their parts at all or sufficiently well, our collective action can fail even if I perform my role. The performance of our play will fail if you are the only one who has memorized her lines. Our conversation will break down if one of us monopolizes it or consistently trolls the others. Our public goods will wither and die if most of us avoid paying our taxes. The best designed classroom learning activities will fail to teach if none of the students has prepared or is willing to take part.

When a college adopts a plan to close racial gaps in graduation rates, it requires the work of multiple people within the institution. Even if a particular faculty member can act in ways that close racial success gaps in her classroom, she is unable to move the needle on graduation rates across the college. The larger collective action requires wider work. If only some do the work required, not only will the plan fail, but those who have acted in good faith to achieve the plan's goals will have their work frustrated.

There is a further and more troubling way my participation in collective actions can be vulnerable to others. Sometimes, the very nature of what I end up doing depends on what my colleagues and collaborators do. In these cases, it isn't merely that my individual action fails to contribute to our reaching our collective goal. Rather, their action so changes what we do that they thereby change what I have done. Their failures don't merely frustrate my attempts; they corrupt them.[8] Consider a college that sets a goal of admitting and recruiting a more diverse student body as part of a commitment to contributing to broader equality of opportunity. Those in the admissions office change how and where they recruit and how they evaluate applications. They succeed in creating an incoming class that is markedly more racially and economically diverse than the college has had in its history. Imagine, however, that there is not sufficient buy-in among those in charge of student life or on the faculty to make the changes that would contribute to the success of this new student body. Many faculty and administrators take the attitude that being able to attend their college is a privilege and anyone afforded that privilege has thereby been offered enough. They don't take themselves to have any further obligations to these new students, and perhaps can't even imagine what those obligations might be. When the new students show up on campus, they find an unwelcoming environment and teaching practices that make assumptions about them that are false. These students end up failing or dropping out or being miserable much more frequently than do the students who resemble the members of previous classes. This is not only terrible for these students; it also changes what the admissions office has done. It turns out not to have afforded a new group of students equal opportunity and access, but to have lured them into a situation where they are likely to be miserable and fail. The admissions officers' actions have been corrupted.

I can try to minimize the vulnerability inherent in collaborative action in various ways. I might find ways to police nonperformance or enact rigid rules and reporting mechanisms that make subversion harder. But, as the literature on social trust suggests, the most effective way to address this vulnerability is by building the resources of social trust: the safety that is created by members of a collective being trustworthy in carrying out their given tasks and roles.

Social trust is generally characterized as the belief that others will fulfill their obligations within a collective scheme. It explains why citizens in some countries generally pay their taxes without a lot of enforcement while citizens in other countries do not. In the former countries, people generally believe (trust) that their fellow citizens will also pay their taxes. When social trust of this sort is widespread, it can act as a form of social capital, a resource for the society to use that grows over time. The more a society or institution is characterized by social trust, the more effective and efficient it can be at carrying out its mission, and the more that effectiveness will inspire further social trust. Societies that lack social trust can find themselves in the opposite spiral, falling into "social traps."[9]

Anthony Bryk and Barbara Schneider, whose book *Trust in Schools* makes the case for social trust as a resource for school improvement, introduce a form of social trust they call "relational trust."[10] Relational trust exists when there is a match between the obligations people in certain roles take on, the expectations people in other roles have, and the fulfillment of these obligations and expectations.[11] So, for instance, there is relational trust between faculty and administrators when the administration does what the faculty expects it to do, and vice versa, and this behavior reflects what each takes their obligations to be. Bryk and Schneider then claim that an individual's judgment that someone is fulfilling those role obligations depends on perceptions of that person as showing them respect, and demonstrating competence, integrity, and a personal regard for others.[12]

Although Bryk and Schneider develop this account for thinking about K-12 schools, many controversies about the functioning of colleges and universities can be seen as turning on this kind of trust, or its lack. When an administration rolls out a Diversity, Equity, and Inclusion initiative in a way that faculty regard as trespassing on their domain or rights or responsibilities, or when the administration fails to defend a faculty member's controversial but appropriate behavior in the classroom, these actions can undermine the relational trust within an institution. Faculty members who treat students in ways that make it clear that they are less than fully welcome on campus or who otherwise fail to show respect for them undermine the trust students have for the faculty. The lack of such trust can turn small missteps or hard decisions into full-blown crises. In the absence of social trust or the generally trustworthy behavior that warrants it, mistakes are more likely to be interpreted as evidence of malicious intent, and hard decisions are likely to be seen as badly or hostilely made. On a campus where Black students feel alienated, an administrator's racially insensitive remark or complaint about a new policy meant to make the campus climate more welcoming only confirms to black students that they aren't welcome. Moreover, in an environment where systematic failures of trustworthiness have persisted, treating violations of role responsibilities as isolated events also erodes trust. Someone who, on the same campus, decries the controversy created by the administrator's remark as overblown and insists on isolating the one remark from the wider climate just provides further evidence to those who don't trust the administration that the administration doesn't understand or care about the underlying problem and is therefore not trustworthy.

Schools and colleges are sites of social trust not merely because they are institutions, but also because they are institutions whose primary mission is to educate. Since the activities of education—of teaching and learning—are essentially collaborative, social trust plays a particularly central role in educational institutions functioning well. If I act in ways that leave my students mistrustful, to the point that they resist being vulnerable in the ways they need to be in order to learn from me, I will not be able to teach them. This frustrates all of our attempts to do what we set out to do when we come into my classroom.

Consider students who are the first in their family to go to college, or to a college like this, or who are unlike the vast majority of their fellow students (whether because of their race, their politics, their economic situation, or their previous schooling). Consider what happens when the school these students attend sends various subtle signals that it is not organized for people like them—by making assumptions about who its students are, the resources they command, or their social circles or background beliefs.[13] In such situations, students are likely to enter classrooms wary of those who teach them, afraid of being found out or misstepping in some way. A teacher whose attitude or actions show that she, like the institution generally, is not thinking of students like them (or, worse, thinks of them only with hostility and derision) reinforces that wariness. These students in classrooms and at institutions that are untrustworthy in these ways need to have their guard up, doing what they can to limit their vulnerability. They may do the work and find a way to get a good grade, but they are unlikely to learn what is being taught.

Although I come back to this point in later chapters, it is worth seeing how social trust in education intersects with the forms of informational trust discussed above. A teacher or institution can be socially untrustworthy by overlooking or tolerating unchecked harms and costs she or it inflicts on others. If colleges impose costs on some of their students by teaching them to inhabit particular informational trust networks, then the very process of educating students bears the risk of making teachers and educational institutions socially untrustworthy. One way in which I failed my former student was not recognizing the costs that learning what I had to teach him risked imposing, and thus not helping him feel safe enough to genuinely learn in my classroom. Though I think that what I taught him was trustworthy, and though I was not derisive about or dismissive of his views or his presence in my classroom, in attempting to teach him what I was teaching him without being mindful of the costs it might impose I was failing to be socially trustworthy to him.

Trust as Entrusting

When we entrust something we value to the care of another, we are vulnerable to loss and perhaps further harm. This is true even when we lend a book to a friend or leave our shirts at the dry cleaner. The person we trust might lose or damage what we have entrusted to them. They might fail to care for it properly in other ways. Consider, then, how much more is at stake when parents entrust to schools and colleges the care of their children, and college students entrust to professors the development of their minds. Parents are expected not only to hand their children over to relative strangers, but to accept that the overall effect of this care will be to change their children in open-ended ways that can't and won't be specified in advance. We wouldn't hand our shirts over to the dry cleaner on such terms! This form of vulnerability helps to explain why sending one's children to school or college, or going to college oneself, can provoke anxiety, especially among those who have little or no experience of what happens in college.

Much of the literature on trust in moral philosophy focuses on this form of trust, often extending it to cover somewhat different kinds of vulnerability.[14] We can try to reduce or eliminate vulnerability that comes from handing over care of someone or something to another by reducing the caretaker's discretion. We can forge explicit contracts or regulations or require oversight and surveillance. In many situations, however, that is neither possible nor advisable. Consider, for instance, cases where the care involved requires expertise we do not possess. When I entrust a surgeon to remove a tumor or repair a ruptured organ, I am unlikely to know how to do it myself. I have to trust her knowledge and leave the particular steps to her discretion. Perhaps I also trust various medical boards and hospital protocols to manage her discretion, but even then I do so without understanding the details of their rules and regulations or their rationales. Sometimes we cannot enumerate the particular steps of care we are handing to another because we are not in a position to know what they are. Sometimes we have to trust experts to discharge their responsibilities with care, competence, and good will.

Nevertheless, when we entrust something of value to the care of others, we generally have some expectations about what that care involves, even if we cannot be explicit about all the details. I expect the surgeon to remove the tumor and as little of the healthy tissue as possible, even if I have no real idea what that entails or how it might best be done. Similarly, we expect that schools and colleges will teach their students, and perhaps teach them certain kinds of things. We expect that they will not harm their students or put them in harm's way, nor exploit them or allow them to be exploited by others. We also may have an idea of what would count as overstepping the boundaries of expected care and treading into areas that are thought of as the preserve of the family, community, or student herself. Failure to care in these ways would count as a betrayal of that trust.

A school that uses discredited methods for teaching reading and thus fails to turn first- graders into readers betrays the trust of those children's parents. So does a college professor who knowingly or negligently teaches inaccurate information, indoctrinates students rather than teaching them, or recruits them to partisan or sectarian causes. Colleges betray the trust of parents, students, and their communities if they aim to convert their students to a given ideology or to spread propaganda. This doesn't mean that a school can't be explicitly organized to promote a particular set of values. It is appropriate and expected that a military academy cultivate the martial virtues, and a seminary the pastoral virtues. A seminary that does not build up the values of the religion in which it trains its clergy betrays their trust in it, just as a military academy that does not prepare its students for the battlefield does. On the other hand, a public college that aims at either of these ends for all of its students betrays the trust placed in it by its students, their parents, and the wider community.

Schools can also betray the trust placed in them through forms of over-care: teaching more than they should. In the US, for instance, it is assumed that public schools will not provide religious instruction. Among the debates surrounding whether and what forms of sex education schools offer, some touch on questions of over-care. Because religion and some range of sexual mores are thought to be the province of families, schools are often thought to overstep their bounds by teaching these subjects in ways that violate families' values.

It might be thought that a college that builds a new informational trust network for some of its students is guilty of such over-care, and this is one way critics who charge higher education with acting in ways they regard as political frame their criticisms.[15] If, however, colleges can't avoid shaping their students' informational trust networks in one way or another, doing so cannot itself be a betrayal of the trust placed in them. Nevertheless, recognizing this third form of trust calls on colleges to take up this task with greater care.

* * *

Schools and colleges depend on all three of these forms of trust: they are entrusted with a collective project that involves the shaping of informational trust networks. They can thus betray trust in many ways. Some of these betrayals also violate or corrupt the essential mission of schools. Different people may be particularly aware of, concerned with, or sensitive to particular forms of these wrongs, and may weigh their harms and wrongness differently. But I would be surprised if anyone reading this book thinks that colleges who do not protect their students from bullying or physical harm, or who aim to indoctrinate, exploit, or convert them, are engaged in defensible behavior. When people defend teachers or institutions against charges of this sort, they aim to show that the charges are false or somehow misdescribe what happened. They rarely insist that the behavior as described was not wrong.

In the case of the shaping of informational trust networks, however, things get more complicated. Education is, in ways I make clear in chapter 3, fundamentally in the business of refurbishing students' informational trust networks. Whereas all sorts of life experience may shape our informational trust networks in ways we do not expect, educational institutions are perhaps unique in that they do so as part of their deliberate aim. In some cases, this process of reshaping also disrupts and reorganizes students' social networks. The people who inhabit the social networks students are led to leave or move away from may view this disruption as a harm. Their vulnerability to that harm generates anxiety about some forms of education. There may be ways for colleges to do this educational work with greater care and concern for those they harm or put at risk, but they cannot respond to this anxiety by ceasing to shape their students' informational trust networks. When they shape their students' informational trust networks in sometimes transformational ways, colleges are not misbehaving or violating or perverting their essential mission. They are doing precisely what they are designed to do.

{3}

The Education of Trust

When a conservative religious student and his father came to my office to complain about a grade, all three types of trust discussed in chapter 2—entrusting, social trust, and informational trust networks—were at issue. I acknowledged and expressed gratitude for the trust the student and his family had placed in me and my university by asking us to educate him. I tried to assure them we would be trustworthy in carrying out that task. I also tried to shore up their relational trust in me as faithfully and thoughtfully carrying out my role as a teacher. I didn't think enough about the social trust he needed in order to be open to learning from me, though. I didn't, for instance, do enough to make him feel safe in my class so that he could be open to being changed by what happened there. Most importantly, I did not then appreciate that the learning I wanted him to do would reshape his informational trust networks in possibly profound ways, or why he and his father might rightly be wary of that result, or the sorts of obligations that placed on me.

This chapter and the next develop the tools that would have provided a better response. They highlight how different the space of higher education looks when we appreciate its effect on students' informational trust networks. This chapter describes how higher education's main pedagogical aims and distinctive features reshape students' informational trust networks, and the distinctive features of the network that many colleges teach their students to build and inhabit. The next chapter takes a closer look at students, and the effects the project unveiled in this chapter has on them and their ties to family and community.

As the argument of this chapter unfolds, it is helpful for us to think of informational trust networks as a set of pipes that connect potential sources of information to each other and to a given person's cognitive processes.[1] When we trust a source, we let the information it generates directly inform our thinking. We attach, as it were, an inlet pipe from that source to our thoughts through which material can flow freely and unchallenged. When we withhold that trust, we question whether the material a source delivers is reliable and should inform our thinking. This adds filters and valves to the pipes that connect us to that source. The informational trust network a person inhabits can thus be imagined as a system of pipes, nodes, filters, and valves. An informational ideology provides criteria for building and shaping that network—which pipes we add and where we install filters and valves. For the most part, the ideology regulates how and whether the nodes and pipes of the informational trust network can be changed. However, changes in the nodes and pipes themselves can generate a shift in the ideology. Sometimes we come to accept a source of information because a person we independently trust recommends it, rather than because it satisfies the criteria our informational ideology lays out. We add nodes to our network that our ideology would reject, and this then puts pressure on the ideology to change. Developing relationships of trust with new people can thus be a powerful force for changing not only various nodes of our informational trust network, but our informational ideologies as well.

My student came to my class holding fairly traditional conservative views about gender roles. I assume that his views were common in his community, and that part of the way he came to hold them was that he trusted members of his community as sources of information. The informational ideology that led him to regard certain community members and authorities as trustworthy primed him to reject arguments made by people he saw as feminist or left-wing or secular. Had I been able to get him to trust me, and thereby the feminist authors we read who challenged his views about gender roles, he might have begun to at least question and think about those views. Even if he ended up reaffirming his belief in the appropriateness and value of traditional gender roles, the directness of that belief would have changed: he would have added a filter to that set of pipes. But at that point he would have begun to build a trust network that was not fully supported by his informational ideology: he would have accepted as worthy of consideration a set of sources and positions that ideology told him to dismiss. That dissonance, in turn, might have then been resolved not by snapping back to his old trust network, but by adjusting his informational ideology to make room for these new pipes and filters.

How Colleges Shape Trust Networks

Three distinctive features of higher education work to shape students' informational trust networks. First, colleges require students to specialize more than they did in high school. College students receive training in a discipline or profession; they are not merely taught a set of basic facts in a field. Second, colleges pride themselves on teaching students deeper and more systematic forms of critical thinking. Finally, colleges expose students to a wider range of people from a wider range of backgrounds than they are likely to meet in high school or in a job they can get straight out of high school (with the possible exception of military service). Students at elite residential colleges come from all over the world to both study and live together, but even students who commute from home to the most isolated and smallest community colleges will meet some people unlike those they met in high school. Colleges pride themselves on all three of these features. They promote them in their efforts to attract students and financial support. An institution devoted to further educating students with a high school diploma that did none of these things would not be recognizable as a college.

It turns out, however, that each of these activities shapes students' informational trust networks in non-trivial ways: they change the sources of information to which students can and do take an unquestioning attitude, and they shape the informational ideologies that guide students' understanding of what makes certain information sources trustworthy. This is rarely if ever the stated aim of colleges or their faculty, and it generally happens without anyone paying direct attention to it. As with informational trust networks themselves, their transformation happens in the background. It is thus worth examining just how this happens.

Training in a Discipline or Profession

To a far greater degree than primary and secondary education, higher education involves specialization. Even in the US, where most undergraduate programs include some form of general education requirement or liberal arts training, students pursuing a bachelor's degree specialize in some field. Training in a discipline or profession involves more than learning the facts and theories that lie within its domain. It also involves learning certain skills associated with that field that make it possible to think well about its subject matter. A history major not only learns more historical facts than she did in high school, or than her roommate who is majoring in biology or her cousin who is studying physical therapy does. She also learns how to think like a historian. In order to think like a historian, she needs to gain a kind of fluency with reliable sources of historical information. Her newfound fluency helps her take in information not only from history textbooks, but also from articles and books written by and for professional historians, as well as (eventually) from primary source material in archives. In gaining fluency she learns not only about the existence of new sources of information and how to find them, but also how to use them *as* sources of information. She learns to, as it were, read these new sources; they become legible to her. Her roommate the biology major learns to read a different set of material: scientific articles, the results and implications of particular experiments, and the readings of the equipment she uses to run those experiments, among other things. Gaining such fluency serves to extend certain pieces of a student's informational trust network.

The claim that disciplinary training expands a student's trust network will strike some readers as confused. After all, part of the history major's training involves developing resources to interrogate and possibly criticize the various sources she uses and to think critically about the information she gathers from them. The history major is not being led to take on trust everything she reads in a work of history; she is, her professors will insist, being taught how to critically assess it. Nevertheless, in order to do that critical work, she must first be able to genuinely access this information *as* information. It is in that step that she builds out her particular network of pipes.

To see how this works, consider a more basic form of fluency: learning to read one's native language. A child who understands and can speak fluently her native language but cannot yet read its written form may see written texts not as texts or even as writing at all, but as meaningless pictures: lines and squiggles on a page, screen, or sign. The first step in learning to read is learning to recognize some marks as writing: as a set of symbols that encode meaning rather than a picture. At this stage, a child can distinguish writing from images, even if she cannot pick out particular letters or ideograms. The next step involves learning to decipher this code. If her language is written with an alphabet, she learns her letters. In learning her letters, she learns to individuate the pieces of the code: to pick out an "a" as different from an "e," but also to see a 12-point "a" in Palatino font on a screen as the same letter (the same piece of code) as a 36-point "a" in Calibri in a picture book. Now she not only sees some marks as writing, but sees that writing as made up of letters. From there, she can learn how letters encode sounds, and then how groups of letters encode words. At this final stage of learning to read fluently, she no longer sees blocks of written text as a set of grouped letters, but instead as a series of recognizable words.

As she develops into a fluent reader new kinds of things become legible to her because she can take the information they provide directly into her thought process. This ability restructures her perception of the world. Whereas before her world was filled with lots of images, some of which were scribbles, now it is filled with both images and texts, and the texts are made up of words. The sense that her world is filled with writing made up of recognizable words is the result of her ability to take written words she encounters directly into her thought process as a certain kind of information, just as you are doing reading this book. Her fluency as a reader means that she doesn't have to sound words out, construct them from letters, or work out how the lines and curves count as letters, as she once did. That lets her take in information by reading: she can attend to the meaning of the words she reads rather than to their material or linguistic form. In doing that, however, she bypasses other thought processes she went through as she was learning to read. In the normal course of things, she doesn't stop to ask whether the scribbles she is seeing as writing are in fact writing and not merely scribbles that resemble writing. She doesn't stop to think about the spelling of the words or whether she is interpreting the font's rendering of the letters correctly. Of course, she can step back and do any of this if she senses that there might be reasons to interrogate the whole process. But in the normal course of things, she takes an unquestioning attitude to the pieces of information she had to learn to input as she developed fluency: not to what the words say, but to the indications that they are in fact words, and which words they are. She has built and connected the pipes that allow her to take in information contained in writing, and that frees her from thinking about the pipes themselves. In fact, she, like you, will now find that it takes effort to see written words not as words, but as either a bunch of letters or mere scribbles. That is simply what it means to be a fluent reader.

A similar process occurs with the development of other forms of fluency and expertise. As we develop expertise in a particular field, we learn to use its tools and read the reports of other experts in fluent ways: we can take on board and think about what the tools reveal and the experts say without having to question or think about the constructions that go into those deliveries of information. The advanced history major reads articles in history journals and uses archives in a way that is different from how a student in a history class in middle school would. She has built out her history pipes, so to speak, with some combination of a richer set of background knowledge, an understanding of disciplinary terms and contexts, and a developed fluency in the use of the historian's tools. As a result, she is better able to think critically about some claims she reads as she studies history. But (and this is the point I am trying to bring into view here) she can only do that because of the large array of information she explicitly or implicitly trusts. Studying history as a history major in college thus extends her trust network. She adds an array of sources and types of experts she was not able to trust before because she was not in a position to access what they had to say. Just as a fluent reader can no longer easily see a page of text in a language she reads as mere scribbles, a fluent historian can no longer see certain kinds of artefacts or archival material as unconnected items not embedded in some historical context. What makes certain kinds of historical fact and analysis legible to her are the pipes she has built out over the course of her education in history. They extend her cognitive reach, but only by directly inputting lots of information into her thinking.

Disciplinary training extends and shapes trust networks even in fields far from the liberal arts and sciences. Someone who studies occupational therapy or obtains a degree in arts administration, public health, or finance learns to read particular sets of data and sensory input as information. A patient's hand movements after injury, the balance sheet of a nonprofit, or an epidemiological survey comes to carry meaning for them in a direct way that it does not for someone not trained in those fields. Their training has added pipes to their cognitive architecture to extend its reach. Since those pipes are just the informational trust network they inhabit, it has thus altered their trust networks.

Moreover, most disciplines and professions share a more or less well-formed informational ideology: a sense of what makes a given source of information trustworthy. Some fields, for instance, place a premium on quantitative over qualitative data, and some do the reverse. Some rely on a core of authoritative texts or canonical authors and some on particular foundational methods. Part of learning to think within a discipline is learning to use its informational ideology, and part of the effect of learning to add the various pipes and nodes the discipline helps its students add to their networks is to find the informational ideology of the discipline comfortable: easy to deploy and treat as merely good sense about what is trustworthy.

This helps to explain the challenges and benefits of interdisciplinary collaboration. What often makes such collaboration difficult is precisely the different sorts of information different disciplines take for granted. People immersed in different disciplines often have a different sense of what is obvious and what requires explanation or justification. What makes interdisciplinary conversation valuable is that it can provide participants a new set of perspectives: a new way of reading the world that makes different assumptions and thus sees different features clearly. This can have the effect of broadening the collective reach of the collaborators while also forcing them to individually revisit their assumptions. It can thus shake up collaborators' overly settled or complacent informational trust networks.

Critical Thinking

If there is anything beyond specialized training that has a claim to be *the* distinctive feature of higher education, it is training in sophisticated forms of critical thinking. Critical thinking involves determining, articulating, and assessing the reasons we have for believing various claims and thus the reasons to trust or not trust various sources of information. Sometimes, examining the reasons for a claim can lead us to be more certain of the information it contains or relies on. At other times, it can lead us to question or stop believing the claim itself or those who make it. Either way, however, the mere fact that we have stepped out of a trusting relationship with a particular source of information to ask questions about it alters the shape of our trust network. Even if we wind up reaffirming the beliefs that are based on that source, we may no longer do so in a trusting way. In those cases, though we do not disconnect this pipe from our thinking, we add a filter or valve between it and our thoughts. In the long term, developing deeper skills of critical thinking results in permanent changes to those networks: removing certain pipes when critical scrutiny leads us to reject them as reliable sources, adding permanent filters to them so that we only accept what they offer us after heightened scrutiny, or even just changing the nature of our confidence in them from unquestioning to reflective.

As I discussed above, one effect of developing expertise in a given field is the ability to question and evaluate claims made in that field's domain, by both experts and nonexperts. The person with a BA in history can better assess both the claims made by historians and the historical claims made in passing by her family members and friends, as well as by journalists, politicians, and public figures. In standing ready to question these sources, she reduces or eliminates her trust in them, at least on those topics. The fact that disciplinary training also equips us with critical thinking skills doesn't undermine the point made above that it extends our trust networks. The training that equips us with new pipes allows our minds to reach further afield in search of information. The expertise we develop in the use of these pipes allows us to also add in new filters further out or along different axes. It changes where in our thinking process we direct our critical scrutiny and what we trust in order to do that.

Finally, good training in critical thinking includes the development of judgment and discernment about when and where to deploy its scalpel and where to add new filters to our cognitive architecture. As we develop that judgment, we are potentially changing the criteria we use to assess the trustworthiness of sources, and thus reshaping our informational ideologies. Removing pipes or adding filters to our cognitive architecture comes with its own costs. The skilled critical thinker knows how to weigh those costs against the benefits of accuracy and reduced vulnerability to manipulation. Even when an education in critical thinking does not amount to merely a wholesale pruning of a student's informational trust network, it nevertheless affects the shape her network has.

New Social Ties

Elite institutions in the US generally draw students from all over the world. But even the most local and isolated community colleges draw students from a wider geographic range than even the biggest of comprehensive high schools. Colleges work hard to draw students to their campus and keep them there beyond the time necessary to attend classes. Offices of student life cultivate and support various opportunities for civic and social interaction amongst their students. They do so because such campus engagement improves student success and retention, and because many students want and value such opportunities. Such efforts to keep students on campus are just as prevalent at colleges where students commute and often continue to live with their parents as they are at residential colleges. The result is that to varying degrees and in varying ways students who go to college meet and are encouraged to interact with a wider range of people than they encountered in high school. They are more likely to meet people who do not share their culture, religion, or set of basic beliefs. They are more likely to meet people whose families are not like theirs in all sorts of ways, and whose interests, tastes, and passions are unfamiliar to them. Some of these encounters are fleeting, a matter of occasionally or even regularly seeing people who look a certain way in the crowds of students moving around campus as they attend classes. Some are more consequential: Students work on lab assignments or discuss class material with others they would not have encountered in their hometown or neighborhood. Some students share a small dorm room, a bathroom, or a dining hall with others whose lifestyle is unfamiliar or who occupy space in a way that no one they previously knew does. Still others make friends and form romantic attachments with people who grew up seeing the world very differently from them, whether because they attend a different church or come from the other side of the tracks, a different part of the country, or across the world.

These new social interactions are not a direct result of the teaching mission of the college. Even if they involve a lot of learning, and many of them happen in classroom settings, they take place alongside rather than as an integral part of the main instructional work of the classroom. If two students in my class on educational ethics alter their trust networks because of a social encounter in the course of working together on an assignment, this is not a direct learning objective of my class. Nevertheless, the range of new social interactions students engage in are the direct result of intentional policies colleges adopt in their admissions, their structuring of student life, their encouragement of campus engagement, and their support for active learning. A school that allows students to self-select into dorms and does nothing to prevent the formation of clusters of rich students on the "party track," or which places various financial obstacles and entry barriers on some courses of study but not others, may have a lot less cross-class interaction amongst its students than a school that works to foster such interaction.[2] Whether colleges adopt these policies for purely economic reasons or in order to support their students' academic success, the interactions they foster push students to learn (out of necessity if not prior interest) to interact with these new people. It may be that all they learn is to accept that people like *that* are sharing their space. But in many of these interactions, students learn how to talk with new people. Colleges generally celebrate this fact, and they should. If they are set up well, colleges allow students to learn as much from their fellow students as from their teachers, both in their classes and, just as importantly, outside them.

The kind of interactions I have in mind are not those formally organized or mandated for the purposes of learning about differences or building up civic abilities. They are not, in the first instance, *about* diversity or inclusion, even if they foster them. Consider, for instance, the experience of working for a semester with a lab partner in a chemistry class. Lab partners are tasked with working together to figure things out: how to design, run, monitor, and report on various experiments. These tasks require that they talk together and rely on one another. Their chemistry class does not explicitly require them to learn about each other, their different backgrounds and worldviews. But they do have to agree on when to meet to work on a lab report, and work out ways to trust each other to share their observations or hold a device steady while the other prepares a specimen. If they can successfully manage the interactions necessary to work well as lab partners, two further developments can follow. First, both come to have experience of people like their lab partner as generally trustworthy and reasonable—someone they can work with, and perhaps, if all goes well, befriend. That may make them more open to taking seriously challenges their lab partner (or someone like them) makes to certain of their unexamined beliefs. The conservative religious student who has been raised to be distrustful of those outside the faith and particularly of secular, urban elites comes to trust her urban, secular lab partner enough to have to reevaluate some of that distrust. Her lab partner, who has grown up with a certain disdain for religious people from rural areas, comes to trust her enough to rethink his assumptions. If they work well together in the lab, then they might find themselves talking after class about things unconnected to their classwork. But now that conversation begins from a level of trust in one another that they didn't previously have. This makes it more likely that they take seriously what the other says. When one of them says something to the other that challenges an unexamined assumption, this can lead the other to revisit that assumption.

Even if their relationship never leaves the lab, their attempts to work together to figure things out about their chemistry assignment will affect their informational trust networks in ways that go beyond the effects of learning chemistry. As they work together on an assignment, each necessarily brings their own perspectives and assumptions to the task. And herein lies the second potential result of their interaction: each one will at times get challenged by the other in ways that they might not have been challenged by someone who shared more of their background and outlook. Since their circumstances both force them to rely on one another and give them (over time) reasons to trust each other, those challenges can lead to reevaluations of the challenged area. That reevaluation, when it occurs, reshapes their informational trust networks.

Our informational trust networks and our social networks are mutually intertwined: what informational sources we trust affects with whom we can form social ties, and the social ties we form shape which sources we trust. The interaction of the lab partners provides an example of how that happens. By learning to talk and genuinely engage with a fellow student whose informational trust network differs from his own, a student alters his network, even if only by opening parts of it up to challenges from new directions. He may take on board part of his colleague's network that he had not previously relied on, or prune parts of his own where it blocks his ability to interact with his colleague. If he has been raised in a completely secular environment, his budding friendship with his religious lab partner or roommate may lead him to be more open to certain kinds of religious claims and values, whether these come directly from his lab partner or from others. If he has been raised in a politically homogenous enclave, he may hear reasons for doubting his political certainties and anchor points from someone he now takes seriously. If she has been raised in a closed cultural environment that accepts a condescending or hostile attitude to members of a different race or ethnicity, she may find that her dinner conversations or classroom discussions with someone from that group force her to question and abandon those beliefs. In this case, it isn't just that her new friend or colleague gives her evidence that those beliefs are wrong or overly broad; it is that she cannot just accept those attitudes as part of her cognitive architecture and engage on equal terms with him.[3]

As with the other features of higher education, the development of new social ties can alter not only the shape of students' informational trust networks but their informational ideologies. Learning to trust someone they previously thought untrustworthy puts pressure on the criteria they initially used to dismiss people like that. Finding ways to speak to someone they work with may require that they find common ground in their criteria for assessing trustworthiness. That might require each of them to adapt their criteria for making this judgment.

The process of going to college is not merely additive; it is not just a matter of acquiring new knowledge or skills. College refurbishes our informational trust networks in potentially subtractive ways as well. More importantly, it can do this even if it does not change the content of our beliefs. Consider, for instance, the student who comes to college from a religious family and community where the teachings of religious authorities are taken on faith and it is inappropriate to subject them to question or critical scrutiny. In the course of her time at college, she is led to raise questions about some or all of those teachings—perhaps as a result of a general incitement to question one's basic assumptions, perhaps as a result of confronting seemingly well-founded positions that challenge or contradict those teachings, or perhaps because she comes to admire a classmate who rejects them. She thus goes from having an unquestioning attitude to those teachings to having a questioning attitude: seeing them as the sorts of sources that can be scrutinized. Even if she, after such scrutiny, comes to agree with the teachings of her religion and affirm her prior beliefs, she is likely to see them in a different light than she once did. Though she still follows and agrees with them, she may no longer trust them.

The Trust Network College Builds

The reshaping of another person's informational trust network is an intimate and awesome task. Once we see that colleges and universities are in this business, we gain a new perspective on a certain kind of anxiety many people feel about going to college or sending their children to college. It turns out that colleges are in fact doing something about which we ought to be wary. That doesn't mean that colleges ought to stop shaping students' informational trust networks. It does mean, however, that they need to earn and deserve the trust of those whom they affect in this way. In order to know if colleges deserve the trust of those whose informational trust networks they reshape, we need to understand not only that colleges reshape trust networks, but also the features of the trust networks colleges help their students build. To do that, we can begin with the characteristic features of the networks inhabited by college graduates.

Consider, then, the kinds of informational sources college graduates tend to rely on to make sense of the world. They are likely to trust mainstream media outlets and newspapers of record, like the *New York Times*, the *Wall Street Journal*, and the *Washington Post* to supply basic day-to-day information. They are also likely to trust the sorts of specialized information that comes from the reports of government agencies devoted to gathering basic social and economic statistics like the Bureau of Labor Statistics and the census, as well as information generated by more academic or scientific sources and published in peer-reviewed journals. These are the sorts of sources one finds quoted in the trusted news outlets as authoritative purveyors of trustworthy information.

Among the things that distinguish these kinds of sources is that those who work for them and produce the information they disseminate are all college educated, and that is part of the reason they are regarded as trustworthy by those who trust them. These sources also present their information in what is understood as a universally legible form, meant to be graspable from any position or perspective. These features of expression are so baked into the ways these institutions present information that we often fail to appreciate them as a distinctive feature, and not just an artefact of communicative speech. A source communicates its information in the requisite general form by using standard rather than colloquial language, standard units of measure, publicly recognizable landmarks and signposts, and widely used narrative conventions and metaphors in the reporting of events. Newspapers report specific events as instances of general kinds by relying on these forms of communication.

To see the distinctiveness of this communicative form, consider other ways information might be communicated. Someone passing on neighborhood news or gossip in a tight-knit community where everyone can count on everyone else having access to certain local, situated knowledge and reference points will use colloquial expressions, local shorthands, and reference to local norms, standards, and ways of counting. Someone attempting to pass on information in a culture that prizes or trusts a certain kind of erudition or the rehearsal of long-standing rhetorical models will present that information embedded in those models or by alluding to key canonical texts.

Information presented in universally accessible generic form purports to be perspectiveless and objective, not simple or legible to nonexperts. I may not be able to fully understand an article in a medical journal or a journal of high energy physics, but that is only because I lack a kind of general knowledge of those fields that anyone could, in principle, acquire. In contrast, the locally embedded and situated information contained in a piece of gossip might only make sense to someone who is also embedded in that social space. It is not meant to be graspable from any perspective or position, nor does its claim to trustworthiness rest on its being objective in virtue of being perspectiveless.

In presenting information this way, a source implies that the information is generated by general, universally applicable methods regarded as "scientific" or "academic," and this is one of the reasons this form of communication is regarded as trustworthy. Although methods that are general and usable across a wide field and are thought to be a path to objective knowledge are not unique to the natural sciences, their use marks a discipline as broadly scientific or academic. These methods are used in qualitative as well as quantitative research, by the ethnographer and the literary critic just as much as by the economist and the medical researcher. Even when the qualitative researcher tries to capture knowledge that is local and place- and time-specific, what allows the material she surfaces into the body of what is regarded by her field as genuine knowledge is that she has uncovered it using such methods: protocols for identifying and interviewing subjects and informants, conducting observations, or embedding oneself within a community. These are the sorts of methods that serve the reporter as much as the anthropologist and generate the reporting in the Metro section as well as the monographs and journal articles produced by academic specialists.

College graduates inhabit informational trust networks that rely on an informational ideology which values broadly scientific thinking in the sense described above. To someone whose informational trust network rests on this ideology, the more information is presented in a generic way and the more it appears to be tied to universal claims or derived from broadly scientific methods, the more it counts as trustworthy. Of course, many people who did not graduate from or go to college also use these sorts of broadly scientific criteria to assess the trustworthiness of sources, and many college graduates do not exclusively use such criteria. Nevertheless, reliance on a broadly scientific informational ideology is characteristic of the ways that college graduates think about the world and assess information. Given the features of a college education discussed above, it is not an accident that this is the case. Training within a discipline is not a matter of accumulating templates of classical form or collections of prophetic truths.[4] It involves learning the generalizable techniques that yield universal, generic sorts of knowledge, even when these are used to uncover specialized features of the world. It involves learning the sorts of general theories that such techniques make possible, and that inform those techniques. It involves learning how to express one's findings in the general idioms of the field so as to communicate them to abstract others who find general forms of expression trustworthy. Instruction in critical thinking of the sort found in many colleges also aims to generate trust in this kind of knowledge: students are taught to check on the generality of knowledge claims and to look at the methods that generate them to make sure they are suitably scientific. Critical thinkers are taught to privilege repeatable over idiosyncratic results and to check for the use of methods designed to produce objectivity rather than to look for the prophetic gifts or moral righteousness of the source, or to compare what it delivers with particular historical forms or templates.

The development and widespread social adoption and approval of this sort of thinking, not only in the natural sciences but also in the social sciences—and, to an increasing degree, even in the humanities—is arguably the great intellectual contribution of the modern university.[5] University researchers rely on this kind of broadly scientific thinking to conduct their investigations, and universities are designed to credential and endorse such thinking and more or less only such thinking as generating genuine knowledge. In turn, it is training in this sort of thinking designed to make a wide range of complex distant phenomena legible that makes up the vast bulk of what is taught in college classrooms.[6] This, in turn, helps to explain why college graduates are likely to inhabit trust networks that rest, at least in large part, on a broadly scientific informational ideology.

To the extent that colleges play a key role in building, supporting, and strengthening this kind of broadly scientific trust network for their students, they benefit those students in several ways. Broadly scientific methods provide a way to find legible and intelligible order amidst the heterogenous buzz of particular phenomena. They provide a means to develop knowledge that, because it is standardized, can be applied across different areas and compared and developed into general theories. Inhabiting such a network can thus greatly extend the reach of one's cognitive powers. It can make much more of the world—both in extent and in depth—legible. Those trained in the methods it endorses can develop powerful theories, global comparisons, and general conclusions that rely on the aggregation of data. Because these methods are generic, they can also be transferred from one realm to another. Students who learn general and transferable methods for reading a play by Shakespeare can use them to unpack the richness of a novel by Toni Morrison or a piece of spoken-word poetry heard at a poetry jam. Students who learn how to interview a subject in a sociology class develop techniques that are useful for reporting the news, developing an opinion poll, or getting to know a new colleague. Coming to comfortably inhabit such a network can thus be thrilling and magical, as whole new areas of the world and human life light up as legible.

Beyond the intellectual benefits, learning to be this kind of knower places one in conversation with other college graduates and thus with the vast majority of people who have access to and control of the major levers of power in the society. When people praise the value of a liberal arts education as equipping them to be able to "talk to anyone," this is the sort of advantage they have in mind.[7] By helping their students build and inhabit an informational trust network that aligns with the trust networks of the advantaged and powerful members of society, colleges confer a social advantage on their students that is, in an important sense, independent of whether this process gives them a better understanding of the world. As we have seen, engaging with others requires that our informational trust networks overlap, and is made easier the more they coincide. Since it is hard to work with people who find us inscrutable, we are unlikely to be hired into or succeed at a job where our coworkers find us so because we inhabit wholly distinct trust networks. Thus, by shaping their informational trust networks to align with those of other college graduates, colleges prepare their students for careers and lives among other college graduates, and thus in the elite sectors of society.

Note, however, that this suggests that one important way a college education benefits those who receive it involves particular processes of social reproduction. Colleges are not merely improving their students' capacities for knowledge; they are fitting them to occupy a particular social class, and reinforcing that class's way of making sense of the world. Colleges might perform this task without intending to: after all, part of what shaped the informational ideologies of previous generations of this part of the workforce is their experience in college. As long as colleges continue shaping students to inhabit this same informational trust network, they will be making sure their new graduates are well molded for the jobs they hope to get.

But insofar as colleges are training their students to easily occupy a particular social class, they are going to end up doing at least two things we might think they should not be doing. First, they will be supporting the processes by which that social class reproduces itself. Since that class also has greater access to economic success, political power, and social influence than other classes, helping it to reproduce itself may help to perpetuate various forms of social inequality in the society. Second, and related, by working to shape, even in the background, their students' informational trust networks to align with those of this elite social class, they impose a burden on students from other classes that they do not impose on students who grew up already in that class. In particular, the transformational effects of college will be more profound and more wrenching for students from non-elite classes who may arrive on campus inhabiting different informational trust networks. These students will have to contend with the very real possibility that succeeding at college will create hard-to-bridge distance between them and their families and home communities. Because getting through college will be easier for children who already occupy this class and its trust networks, using college as a gateway to this influential and well-supported part of the economy will end up helping members of this advantaged social class pass on their privileges to their children. Colleges' complicity in this kind of social reproduction would be independent of the many other ways colleges in a system like that in the US serve to perpetuate social and economic inequality:[8] it would be baked into what and how they teach. While it may be the case that parents and students from other classes who must bear these costs would be willing to do so in order to access the advantages that come from joining this class, they will not thereby come to trust that process. One result of that non-trusting acceptance will be resentment among those who are not part of the college-educated class toward those who are and the institutions that form them and the trust networks they inhabit.

Note that these effects would not be due to the particular content or the value of the trust networks colleges end up helping students inhabit. It might turn out that the trust networks inhabited by college graduates and into which they are initiated are highly trustworthy as paths to knowledge, and more so than any of the other networks widely inhabited by other members of the society. Nevertheless, the process of social reproduction at play here, and the ways this is guided by the aim of preparing students for a particular set of social roles, is going to shape the trust network being built and the ways colleges bring students to inhabit it. In particular, it is going to tend to insulate this broadly scientific trust network from external challenges and new resources even as the population of college graduates becomes more diverse in other ways. It will also make the process of getting a college education easier for some students while imposing costs on others. I explore those costs in chapter 4.

{4}

The Social Cost of a College Education

Discussions of the high and rising costs of college tend to focus on direct economic costs: the price of tuition and associated fees, the opportunity costs in lost wages, and the expense and wisdom of public programs to offset those costs. Beyond these economic costs, many students pay a psychological price to make it through college. College can trigger or exacerbate common mental illnesses like severe anxiety and depression, and this can impose costs on the students who suffer in these ways and the families who care for them. Some groups of students bear a different kind of psychological cost that comes from having to spend time in an environment that is foreign or even unwelcoming to them. The student culture at highly selective schools, formed as it is by a high percentage of the very wealthy, tends to be both alienating and unaffordable for poor and working-class students, as well as for many minoritized students.[1] Students of modest means often find it disorienting to move to a social environment where their peers have access to large amounts of disposable spending money for expensive meals, clothes, and trips. Many colleges are also set up in more subtle ways to reward students who have the skills and attitudes wealthier kids develop as they are groomed for college. These include the willingness to speak up with confidence in class, show up at faculty office hours to ask for help, and call on a pool of cultural knowledge that professors recognize. It also includes the social skills, motivation, and comfort level necessary to get to know professors well enough to get good letters of recommendation from them. When faculty just assume that all of their students have these skills (and so reward certain forms of class participation, don't explain what "office hours" are, etc.), they end up further advantaging their advantaged students and comparatively disadvantaging their disadvantaged students. More tangibly, even when colleges provide scholarships for their poorer students, they often charge fees that are prohibitive for these students for everything from attending campus cultural events and joining certain clubs to accessing exams and programs that are gateways to particular degrees.[2]

Many students also face what Jennifer Morton calls "ethical costs" to go to and succeed in college.[3] Students who come from families where older children are expected to be available for the care of younger siblings or older relatives may find that they are forced to choose between family responsibilities and dedication to classwork. Even when poorer students succeed despite all these obstacles, they often face choices that their richer classmates do not. The interesting, well-paying jobs for which college is supposedly the gateway are, by and large, located not in the communities in which they grew up, but in the sorts of places their richer classmates did. Due to the geography of economic opportunity, poorer students often have to choose between reaping the benefits of their education and staying close to their families and the communities in which they grew up. These are the kinds of dilemmas that confronted Todd, whom we met briefly in chapter 1, and led him to remark that "it was almost like I was given the choice . . . to sacrifice relationships for being able to survive college."[4] This list of costs doesn't even begin to include those imposed by the microaggressions many minoritized students experience from white classmates, professors, and staff, the overall whiteness of many academic disciplines and spaces, or the shamefully high levels of sexual assault and harassment on many campuses.

As these examples suggest, the psychological and ethical costs some students bear to go to, stay in, and graduate from college are neither fairly distributed nor easily compensated. They play an important role in making the experience of college more difficult, risky, and costly for certain students. For the most part, the costs surveyed above result from features of college that are ancillary to the education it provides, especially in its classrooms. Colleges can mitigate many of these costs by changing their campus cultures, providing non-stigmatizing subsidies for their poorer students,[5] and offering them other sorts of non-academic support. None of that requires changing what or how they teach. As we have seen, however, a college education shapes students' informational trust networks. Since a person's informational trust network and her social network are related, the very process of becoming educated can place strains on some students' social ties. This suggests that the very education college provides imposes a further social cost on at least some students. This chapter explores those costs.

The Social Cost of Being Educated

Tara Westover grew up in a survivalist family living on a mountainside in Idaho that rejected, among other things, formal education and medical care. In her memoir, *Educated*, she recounts her journey from there to BYU and then to graduate school at Cambridge. As she gains an education, she comes to a new view of the world that is incompatible with that of her parents and some of her siblings, and this leads her to become increasingly estranged from them, until she finally breaks ties with them completely. At one turning point in that process she describes the effect of the classes she took during a semester of her junior year: "For four months I attended lectures on geography and history and politics. I learned about Margaret Thatcher and the Thirty-Eighth Parallel and the Cultural Revolution; I learned about parliamentary politics and electoral systems around the world. I learned about the Jewish diaspora and the strange history of *The Protocols of the Elders of Zion*. By the end of the semester, the world felt big, and it was hard to imagine returning to the mountain, to a kitchen, or even to a piano in the room next to the kitchen."[6]

While Westover's childhood was extreme and unusual in many ways, this description of college is, and is meant to be, familiar. Going to college exposes students to a much wider world than they are used to, even if they are used to a world quite a bit wider than Westover was. In Westover's case, college offered her entry into a world that was an escape from an abusive family, and so it can seem obvious that her widened horizons would have this effect and that the change would count as an unmitigated gain. But Westover is making a different point here. First, she is claiming that it was *because* college had made the world feel very big that it was hard to imagine going back home. Second, she is trying to keep track of the losses involved as well: although her education made it easier to escape a bad situation, it also made it harder to imagine returning to a place she knew and, in many ways, loved. Those are more puzzling claims, even if they express a familiar sentiment. Why should a sense of the world as very large rule out a return to one's home, a space one knows and loves? Some students can't imagine going home again after college because in college they have found an unambiguously better life—safer, more affirming, and more economically advantageous. But that is not the case for all students who can't imagine returning home. For some of them, the choice is less clear. The analysis offered so far can help us make sense of those students' experience.

An education that transforms some students' informational trust networks inevitably reshapes their social networks in ways that can strain their ties to home and family. Whether it does so, however, depends on the distance between the informational trust networks students inhabit when they begin college and those they inhabit when they leave. Some students arrive at college already inhabiting trust networks much like the one college helps them build. For them, a college education smooths the rough edges, expands its reach along specific dimensions, and maybe brings the whole network into greater coherence. These students improve their trust network as a tool for knowing about the world, without radically transforming it. The social ties they had prior to college come under little strain from this process. These students tend to come from households filled with and surrounded by people with college educations: not only their parents and friends, but also their parents' friends, neighbors, and colleagues and their friends' parents, neighbors, and colleagues. Given the demographics and history of higher education in the US, such students are likely to be whiter, richer, and more socially advantaged, and less likely to be from rural areas, than the average eighteen-year-old.

Other students enter college with informational trust networks that are very different. For these students, college engages in a transformation somewhere between a gut-and-rehab and a tear-down-and-rebuild of their trust networks. These are the students college transforms most completely, and their social networks are thus most likely to be drastically altered in the process. When this alteration of their trust networks makes it harder for them to return home, the very process of getting a college education imposes social costs on them and those they leave behind that it does not impose on their more advantaged peers. We can appreciate the differential effects of learning to inhabit a broadly scientific network by considering some of the variety of informational trust networks students inhabit when they arrive at college.

The Students Colleges Teach

The descriptions below aim to capture characteristic features likely to be found amongst certain demographics. They are idealized sketches, not exercises in armchair sociology. In reality, most people's informational ideologies are more mixed, and the workings of their trust networks are more fragmented than these sketches suggest. In addition, the effect of growing up in any of these sorts of communities can have varying effects on how a person thinks about and interacts with the world, even before colleges get involved. In distinguishing between the children of college-educated professionals and those who grow up in rural communities, religious households, and marginalized communities, I don't mean to imply that these are wholly distinct populations—that there are, for instance, no religious college graduates from marginalized groups who live in rural communities, or that no religious people in a marginalized community who have not gone to college lead their children to trust many of the kinds of sources that make up a broadly scientific informational trust network. The communities described below overlap and intersect in various ways, and people who grow up in more than one of them are likely to have trust networks that include features of more than one of these informational ideologies. In fact, nothing in the argument that follows depends on any particular feature of each portrait being accurate or widely prevalent in the demographic in question. Nevertheless, I draw these sketches here to make plausible three general points: (1) that there are trust networks other than the broadly scientific one that have a claim to providing reasonable insight about the world; (2) that different students pay different social costs as a result of their college education because of the sorts of trust networks inhabited by those they leave behind; and (3) that members of some communities might reasonably see the networks a college education builds as something other than an obvious improvement.

Children of College-Educated Professionals

Many students, especially at more selective and prestigious colleges, have college-educated parents and inhabit communities where all or almost all the adults have college degrees. Their parents work in the sorts of professional jobs where most of their colleagues also have college degrees, and so they grow up in the sorts of suburbs and cities where these jobs are found in large numbers. Though they live in particular cities or suburbs that mark them in small ways and differentiate them from their college classmates from other cities and suburbs, the places they come from are not so different from one another. The students who grew up in the Midwest will drink "pop" while those from the East Coast will drink "soda." When students from Boston end up going to college in Chicago, they learn to ride the "El" but that only involves minor adjustments from their experience with the "T." The places in which these students grow up have many features in common: they have a pretty high rate of in- and out-migration and a fairly standard set of features, cultural opportunities, and geographies. Students from one of these places would be able to find their footing relatively easily in their classmates' hometowns.

Though these communities often contain racial, ethnic, and religious diversity, the particular neighborhoods these students grow up in and the schools they attend have much less class diversity. Even if the particular mix of religions, ethnicities, and races differs from place to place, these neighborhoods tend to contain and value a relatively uniform set of diversities. More importantly, their schools, families, and neighbors primarily teach these students to trust the sorts of broadly scientific sources discussed in chapter 3. As a result, even if these students vary in many ways in their political and religious beliefs, their cultural tastes, and their professional and intellectual interests and ambitions, they grow up being prepared to talk to one another, and they find each other and their respective upbringings completely legible.

When these students go to college, they already inhabit a trust network that significantly overlaps the trust networks of their teachers and most of their similarly advantaged classmates. It is a network not altogether different from the one an education in broadly scientific methods builds out for them. College extends the reach of their trust networks along some dimensions and may lead them to question some sources of information that their parents trust. Nevertheless, these changes result from the sorts of thinking and reflection that their parents also use to work out what and whom to believe. When colleges teach those students to inhabit a broadly scientific trust network, their new trust network relies on the same ideology as the network they held previously. Even if college transforms them, and they graduate from college with political, moral, or religious views different from those with which they began, or those they previously shared with their families, this doesn't render them strangers to their parents. Even if they end up settling in a new place after college, nothing in these features of their background prevents them from maintaining ties to the communities from which they came. Whatever costs these children pay to go to college, they rarely involve the straining or severing of their pre-college social ties.

Students from Rural Communities[7]

Small towns in rural parts of the US are often more ethnically, racially, and religiously homogenous than cities and suburbs. Their schools, however, often contain more class diversity. (An isolated small town may only have one public school and no nearby alternatives to the public school system, so that all its children, regardless of class background, attend the same school.) Small towns experience much less in-migration, and this makes possible forms of information exchange that rely on local knowledge and expression. Even when they are not hostile to newcomers, people in such towns may have developed ways of sharing information that is not easily graspable or available to

outsiders. Markers of status, local reference points, and various local
norms and customs may require a kind of situated knowledge and experience that outsiders don't have and can't acquire easily. This serves
to draw the boundaries of the community more tightly, but it also in-
fluences the sorts of information sources people in the town regard as
trustworthy and the signals of trustworthiness they respond to. Their
trust networks are likely to be populated with at least some hyper-
local institutions and authorities whose claims to trustworthiness
stem from that local connection. Within such trust networks, signaling insider status by using local idioms or referring to highly situated
knowledge increases one's perceived trustworthiness. On the other
hand, relying on the idioms of general, scientifically acquired knowledge marks you as an outsider who is less likely to be trustworthy.

Children who grow up in this kind of environment develop trust
networks that include holders of local knowledge and authority,
possibly alongside but also possibly to the exclusion of those whose
knowledge is more general and tied to the sorts of scientific institutions that populate the trust networks of college graduates. They may
grow up hearing about the foolishness or arbitrariness of distant bu-
reaucrats armed with regulations and formulae that don't apply well
to a local situation. They may learn how to farm a particular piece of
land, run a particular business, or ply a particular trade not so much
by applying general theories to it as by apprenticing with farmers,
business owners, or tradespeople who have long experience doing
that work in that place. They may hear stories of the time someone
came to town with lots of book learning about how to farm and the
disaster they unleashed on those who followed their advice. They may
learn to be skeptical of outside experts who think they know better.
The knowledge that shows its value to them is situated, not general,
and its claim to trustworthiness comes precisely from its situatedness. If they are paying attention, they develop a deep knowledge of
their local environment and social networks that does not so easily
generalize to other people and places. Whereas a college education
teaches students to trust scientific methods and information that is
general and knowledge that is transferable across contexts, the trust
networks children build in rural communities may take the generality
and transferability of forms of knowledge as reasons for distrust, and

the situatedness and non-transferability of other forms of knowledge as reasons to trust them. Their trust networks rest on an ideology that values long experience and close involvement rather than general scientific methods. Relying on such trust networks is not a result of ignorance or failure to grasp the information offered by scientific sources; instead it is often the result of appreciating the specific features of a local context that are often elided in the production of scientific theory or general rules. They know and understand the very sorts of locally relevant details that are overlooked or ignored by general theories and the distant state agencies that rely on them. And this situated knowledge provides grounds for mistrusting the state and its various scientific agencies when these can't see or attend to the information that gives sense and meaning to their lives.

Students from Religious Households

In many rural places, religion and religious institutions play a large role in community life; for this reason this category and the previous one comprise overlapping populations. I separate them here because being raised in a very religious household can shape a person's trust networks in different ways than growing up in a rural community can, and because many people who grow up in religious households do not live in rural communities. Rural communities develop trust networks that place a premium on situated knowledge and local experience. Religion offers a different informational ideology. Members of a close-knit religious community build informational trust networks whose nodes are supported by religious authority. That can involve several kinds of tests. Some sources, like the Bible, Qur'an, or Torah, are regarded as trustworthy based on their claim to divine provenance. Religious officials are trusted because of their position, or their deep knowledge of and involvement with the religion's traditions and teachings. In addition to direct religious backing, certain forms of moral righteousness are also often taken as indicators of trustworthiness. Some sources of information are deemed trustworthy because of their own religious devotion or righteous character, whereas others are distrusted because they are seen as having a low or corrupt moral character. The more all-encompassing a person's religious tradition, the more his trust network will be infused with and supported by religious criteria, and the more it will come into conflict with the conceptual frameworks and findings of a broadly scientific network.

Students who come to college from a religious tradition that confines itself to a small set of ritual practices and personal moral beliefs may be more able to integrate these aspects of their trust networks with one that rests on a broadly scientific ideology. Their particular manner of prayer does not come up for discussion in their classes, and they do not expect religious authority to be a possibly competing source of information about US history, the structure of chemical bonds, or even gender roles. The ungodly behavior of a professor or other source is not taken as a sign that what she says about her area of expertise is untrustworthy. Students who grow up in a more all-encompassing religious tradition, on the other hand, may have more difficulty fitting their religiously supported trust network together with those they are asked to develop in college. They may find that their trusted religious sources are not accepted as valid in classroom discussions or papers, and that they must learn to inhabit trust networks that rely on sources that directly conflict with religious authorities. Perhaps more importantly, they need to learn new and possibly incompatible criteria for judging the trustworthiness of sources. Rather than looking to religious approval or signs of religiously approved virtue, they need to attend to the signs of scientific thinking, expression, and proper methodology. A student who makes this shift successfully may find herself disagreeing with those back home about particular factual claims. More importantly, she may find that her ways of pursuing that disagreement are foreign to the way people from her home community make sense of the world: they do not recognize her newly acquired moves in conversation as legitimate. If she develops the new informational trust network college shapes for her, she will find it increasingly hard to talk with those back home.

Students from Marginalized Communities

For reasons innocent and not so innocent, many communities' experience with government agencies, statistical studies, government policy, and scientific communities is not positive. They have been harmed by "rational" policies or because the state has overlooked what was important to them, rendered it invisible, and then bulldozed it—often literally. They have been targeted by state violence and control in the name of public safety and order. Their land has been torn up or poisoned or paved over in the name of economic development and opportunity. Their cultures and ways of life have been pushed to the margins or even out of existence in the name of modernity, civilization, and progress. While this includes many rural and religious communities, it also includes various minoritized communities, both rural and urban. People who grow up in such communities are likely not to regard the agencies that harmed them as trustworthy sources of information. They are also likely to distrust the findings of scientific panels and research, and of the university-based public policy programs on which these agencies rely in making their decisions. This distrust extends beyond rejecting the particular information these sources deliver. As with the person who has grown up learning to trust situated knowledge precisely on the grounds of its situatedness, the person who grows up learning to distrust certain official government sources learns to distrust them not only for what they say and have justified in the past, but based on their form and grounding. If governments and large corporations speak the language of science, economic modeling, growth, and aggregating statistics, and then go on to do great harm to places and people you know and love, these do not become markers of trustworthiness, even as information. Members of communities harmed in these ways are thus likely to develop trust networks that rest on a different ideology: one that values solidarity with the community. A student who has learned the lessons her community has learned from its experience may, along with them, only trust those who explicitly recognize the needs of her community and how those have been overlooked or thwarted in the past. She may very well come to college primed to distrust not only many of the sources her teachers regard as trustworthy, but also the sorts of grounds and markers her teachers rely on to vouch for the trustworthiness of those sources. If she demands assurances of more than good will and unbiased treatment before trusting the sources of information her teachers trust and rely on, they may regard her demands as calls for special treatment or the result of a failure to distinguish objective investigation of the world from the pursuit of political agendas.

As with children from the other two groups, if a student from this type of background holds fast to the trust network she arrives with, she may find college an unwelcoming, possibly hostile environment—one that speaks in the tones and idioms of those who have harmed her community. She may find that the voice and outlook she brings to her classes and discussions cannot gain a foothold or hearing. If, on the other hand, she is persuaded or pressured to give up the trust network she grew up inhabiting to succeed in learning what college has to teach her, then her community may regard her as having betrayed it and its knowledge and interests. Coming to inhabit the broadly scientific trust network that a college builds for her can strain the social ties she had when she enrolled. She thus also faces a set of social costs that the children in the first group do not face.

The Social Costs of College Education

For a student who begins college occupying the sorts of trust networks that develop in the final three kinds of community, a college education can be not only a deeply transformative experience, but a deeply disorienting one: such a student learns not only to trust a whole range of sources that have been excluded from or disvalued by the trust networks of her home community, but also to distrust the value of the kinds of knowledge she has previously relied on. It is not just that she exchanges the items in her trust network for new sources. She is asked to change the criteria she uses to determine whether a source is trustworthy or not, the very ideology on which her informational trust network is built. The qualities that signaled trustworthiness before now raise skepticism, and the qualities that garnered skepticism now count as reasons for trust. A college education that leaves her with a broadly scientific worldview equips her to take her place in the social networks occupied by other college graduates, but it may make her unintelligible to her family and her family unintelligible to her. It is likely to put strains on her social ties to her home and her home community, as she no longer shares large portions of their trust network. This change may reveal itself in a different set of beliefs or views on moral, political, and religious matters, but it need not. Trust networks don't fully determine beliefs. She can fundamentally alter the shape of the trust network she inhabits without changing her moral, religious, and political positions. And even if she does change her beliefs, this is not the ultimate reason for her strained social ties. The problem goes deeper.

The strains a college education can place on some students' social ties imposes costs on them that other students may not face. This cost cannot be offset with scholarships or debt relief, and it cannot be completely mitigated by reshaping the social life colleges foster. It is built into the kind of education colleges and universities provide, even those aspects of that education they have very good reason to provide. Moreover, these costs are not borne by the students alone. Insofar as they involve strained social ties, the costs are borne as much if not more by the communities in which these students grew up. These communities not only lose beloved children; they often lose those who have the most talent and drive. Even if some of these students do not see their strained social ties as a loss and are happy to escape a community they found oppressive or just overly narrow, those they leave behind pay a price in losing them.[8]

Because of these costs, many students from such communities either choose not to go to college or do not thrive while there. If they start college, their experience often serves to reinforce the difference in their minds between their own trust networks and those of distant elites, and the attractions of what they know. They may decide that the costs aren't worth paying, and so forgo all the other advantages society ties to a college degree. In many cases, that experience also saddles them with economic burdens: the often catastrophic combination of sizable debt and unimproved earning potential faced by those who start but don't complete college.[9]

The social costs listed above come in degrees. My portraits of rural, religious, and marginalized communities laid out ideal types to emphasize the differences. In actual fact, however, students from these places arrive in college with trust networks that have a variety of sorts of elements and may not be fully unified by a single coherent informational ideology. A great deal of their primary and secondary education will have begun to build the elements of a broadly scientific trust network for them. To the extent that this is the case, the costs students bear in college will be less pronounced. Not all these students find, like Tara Westover, that the cost of their education is a complete break with their parents. For some, the costs will be measured in less easygoing dinner conversations or a need to learn to code-switch or maintain two somewhat divergent ways of being: one for the home spaces they grew up in and one for the spaces they now inhabit.[10] For others, it means expending extra effort to knit together a set of disparate and ill-fitting social ties. For many, it means a longer or harder period of adjustment to find their bearings at college and then to find them again when they return home. Nevertheless, these are costs some students bear to go to college—costs that come from the education they receive, and how it trains them. They are the sorts of costs I failed to address in my conversation with my student and his father, and for which, at the time, I had no good remedies or justifications.

Debating College's Costs and Benefits

Students who accurately perceive the social costs their education imposes and nevertheless attempt to maintain their social ties may find their efforts overwhelmed or rebuffed in various ways. They may find the campus culture and the curriculum to be unwelcoming, and perhaps hostile. Parents who watch their children's thinking processes change in ways that strain their prior social connections may have a hard time seeing what is happening to their children as a process of education and improvement. They may come to see colleges as places of indoctrination rather than education. Progressive criticism that charges colleges with not being sufficiently inclusive, and conservative criticism that raises charges of indoctrination, both give voice to these perceptions. Critics who make these charges and those who defend higher education against them often seem to be talking past one another, each failing to appreciate the points the other is making. The critics point to the social costs of a college education, and the defenders to its benefits, as if these have independent causes. We can now see, however, that both sides are pointing to the effects of the same source: the way a college education trains students to inhabit a broadly scientific trust network.

Many supporters of higher education who defend it against charges about exclusion and indoctrination implicitly point to the value of such a network in knowing about and understanding the world around us. The sources that make up this trust network are, in many ways, trustworthy and reliable in providing genuine and true information about the world. Working within it not only adds to our mass of knowledge, but increases our understanding. Supporters thus argue, in effect, that by building a broadly scientific trust network for their students, colleges are making students better thinkers and knowers—educating them. They also claim that by making students better thinkers and knowers, a college education positions them to participate in and benefit from the economic, technological, and scientific advances brought about by a reliance on this network. From this perspective, even if some students face the sort of social costs mentioned above, they ultimately benefit from paying that cost: they shed untrustworthy informational networks for more trustworthy ones. This case is not unimpeachable, and we will need to think about its shortcomings below. But it does point to an important benefit of inhabiting this trust network.

Critics, in contrast, focus on the social role this informational trust network and its ideology play. They point to the fact that this network is the one inhabited by most college-educated people, who in turn make up the segments of US society—in government, business, academia, media, and culture—that set agendas and decide what kinds of knowledge counts and whose perspectives get taken seriously. It is thus also the network inhabited by those who grow up in the communities and neighborhoods where they live. Whatever its value for knowing about aspects of the world, the critics point out that it is not a network that all communities inhabit. This makes more apparent the costs to both students and their communities of learning to inhabit this broadly scientific network. Critics pay attention to the social costs paid by those outside the circle of the college-educated and point to the overlooked value of the trust networks those communities inhabit. They see training designed to enable students to inhabit a broadly scientific network not as making better knowers and thinkers, but as reproducing the thought patterns of a segment of society to which they or those for whom they claim to speak do not belong. From this perspective, those who defend what colleges teach are not only justifying imposing this cost on other people's children and their communities, but doing so in a way that denies those community members' capacities as knowers. These critics and those whose anxieties they give voice to do not hear a stirring defense of the power of particular methods of knowledge discovery and production in this defense of higher education. Rather, they hear the sort of condescending justification that aristocrats, colonizers, and elites of all stripes have historically used to bolster their own position and power at the expense of those over whom they rule.

Defenders of higher education could avoid this stance if they could learn to appreciate the value of alternative informational trust networks as genuine and fruitful paths to knowledge. In describing the informational trust networks inhabited by children from rural, religious, and minoritized communities, I tried to make clear how they can yield insight into what sources of information are genuinely trustworthy, even if they make judgments about this different from those that would be made by a broadly scientific network. Not surprisingly, they attend to cues regarding the trustworthiness of sources of information that a broadly scientific network is prone to ignore or overlook. It can thus help to dwell briefly on the blind spots a broadly scientific outlook can generate.

The Pitfalls of Scientific Thinking

Scientific thinking is the process of finding legible order amidst the variety of particular phenomena. Its power as a path to knowledge lies there. But the adoption of a broadly scientific informational ideology and trust network can steer us wrong when it licenses blindness to what of value and importance might be lurking in that variety. Making the world broadly legible through these scientific methods is only one way of making sense of the world, of reading one's social and natural environment. It is not merely what happens when one improves the trustworthiness of one's trust network—it is a particular way of doing so.

As the anthropologist James C. Scott's work illustrates, when those with influence and power rely on broadly scientific thinking without appreciating what it overlooks, even their most well-meaning and progressive projects can fail, and fail spectacularly at that.[11] Scott's analysis starts from the recognition that for a person or institution to pursue their aims and plans effectively, the domain in which they act must be legible to them. Scribbles on a page are legible to a reader if she can see them as text and thus decipher the meaning they encode. The legibility of the scribbles allows her to take on and think about the information they transmit. Scott is interested in what makes features of the world like the pattern of land occupation and use in a village legible to a central state bureaucracy. Large central bureaucracies require uniformity and standardization for legibility. They can't make sense of lots of different local practices each with their own rules, units, and standards, or compare them across the breadth of their jurisdiction. States solve this problem by imposing standardization on various otherwise diverse practices—of, for instance, land tenure, the use of weights and measures, and the formal recognition of certain types of civil status and social relations. Doing so facilitates the state's ability to pursue its projects: to levy taxes, regulate behavior and transactions, and conscript soldiers. While standardization increases the legibility to the state of different social practices, it often decreases the legibility for local participants in those practices. Local, organically developed processes are generally legible to those who grew up and lived within them, even if they are opaque to the central bureaucracy. In contrast, the standardization that makes these social practices legible to the state often makes little sense to people who have developed situated knowledge appropriate to their corner of the world.

The relevance of this observation to the pitfalls of broadly scientific thinking is that such thinking supports both the process of standardization and the failure to recognize the costs it imposes. Scott illustrates this dynamic with a brief history of scientific forestry.[12] In eighteenth-century Prussia, as in many European kingdoms, the monarch, and thus the state, owned a lot of land, including a lot of forest. The state's main interest in its land was the revenue it generated. In the case of the forest, that income derived from harvesting timber, so what ultimately interested the state about the forest was the quantity of available timber that might be harvested from year to year. Moreover, the state needed information regarding timber yields that was general across all of its holdings: its inventory of each acre of forest had to yield comparable data so that the data could be aggregated. Scientific forestry was born of this need. It begins with the development of general methods for surveying forests for their trees. These techniques begin to make the forests legible to the state: what had been an incomprehensible resource becomes quantifiable. This "scientific" view of the forest was general in its reach and provided data that could then be thought about, theorized, and used for further purposes. It was generic, and so could be used to compare different forests and include their resources under a single category. It generated the kind of information that a broadly scientific trust network would see as trustworthy.

But this process of calculating a forest's value ignores many important details of how a forest functions and the value it provides for agents other than the state. It ignores the sorts of information about particular forests that local forest-dwellers rely on, as well as what the forest contains and supports beyond its harvestable trees. Though scientific forestry expanded the state's ability to know some things about its forests, it occluded from view other valuable information, and dismissed as unscientific the sorts of heterogenous information that might only pertain to particular forests or their inhabitants. Occupying this informational trust network gave the state and its agents confidence to act on what they saw, even if what they saw turned out to be limited. This confidence led to the scientific management of forests. Scientific forestry attempted to manage rationally the one resource that was of interest to and legible to the state and did so by transforming the forests into its vision of them. Basically, it remade forests into standardized tree farms: rows of evenly spaced trees of a single species and identical age, easy to count, monitor, and harvest efficiently. For reasons that did not become clear for a rather long time, given how long it takes trees to grow, this turns out to be a disastrous way to grow trees. In this sense, scientific forest management turned out to be based on bad science. But even before this became clear, and independently of this failure, it had the effect of destroying all the other ways people and other living things used and interacted with particular forests—not because it rested on bad science, but because it rested on a trust network that dismissed sources of information that couldn't be rendered properly generalizable. When colleges build broadly scientific trust networks for their students, they can impose social costs on those who do not arrive on campus inhabiting such networks. But if Scott's analysis of the role of such thinking in the myopic vision of many central bureaucracies is right, then the social costs of this educational project will be felt even further afield.

If the analysis that has unfolded over the previous four chapters is right, then it is not enough for colleges and universities to insist that they are engaging not in indoctrination but merely in education, or to adopt extracurricular practices to make their campuses more welcoming. A different kind of response is needed that takes the anxiety many feel about college and its sources seriously. In chapters 5 and 6 I offer some suggestions of what that might look like. Chapter 5 constructs an alternative informational trust network that colleges could build, one that would balance out the costs a college education imposes while nevertheless capturing the benefits and avoiding the pitfalls of scientific thinking. Chapter 6 offers some ways in which colleges that took on that task could both inspire and earn the trust of their students and their students' families and communities.

{5}

What Colleges Could Do, Part 1

FOSTER OPEN-MINDEDNESS

College ought to be in the business of making its students better knowers, not merely better at occupying a particular informational trust network. Being a "better knower" involves knowing more: more facts, more theories, more techniques for doing this or that. In most cases, however, and certainly in the higher reaches of education, it also means being better at the activity of knowing itself: both gaining knowledge and discerning genuine and valuable knowledge from falsehoods and trivialities. Someone who is better at knowing is someone who knows more of what matters and knows it more fully, surely, and stably. For instance, she not only knows a bunch of isolated facts about a topic, but also understands how they relate to each other and how as an ensemble they carry meaning or express deeper truths. She can more effectively take in or think critically about new pieces of information, and she can see more clearly what she still needs to find or figure out to answer a question or solve a problem.

We don't become better knowers by relying less on trust to arrive at knowledge. The aim of becoming a better knower is to become less vulnerable to mistakes and manipulation without drastically curtailing our cognitive reach. It thus does not involve replacing all our trusted informational sources with new sources we can rely on without trusting. Nor does it involve installing valves and filters everywhere, so that we check all the information we encounter. We lack the cognitive capacity for that, and even where we can spare some capacity for heightened scrutiny that process comes with its own costs.

Cognitive bandwidth we devote to scrutinizing informational inputs is cognitive bandwidth we cannot use to think with that information. So, making students into better knowers requires helping them inhabit informational trust networks that improve their knowing.

In order to undertake this work without provoking the sorts of anxiety that arise from building broadly scientific informational trust networks, colleges first need to be able to make a convincing case to others that they in fact make students into better knowers. That requires having a characterization of what makes someone a better knower that people who inhabit a wide variety of informational trust networks could accept. Since our particular informational trust networks shape what we claim to know, people who inhabit different networks tend to have very different ideas about what makes someone a better knower. We are all likely to think that people who occupy informational trust networks very different from ours will become better knowers by thinking more like us: we conflate being a better knower with inhabiting our trust network. People who teach in colleges and universities, and thus have spent their whole lives thinking about how to be better knowers, are particularly liable to such conflation. But we can't just assume that the cognitive architecture of certain people (say, those who are college educated or experts in various fields) is better at generating genuine knowledge. That, after all, is what we are trying to figure out. And we have plenty of historical examples of experts and highly educated people being systematically wrong about important topics. (We also have many historical examples of nonexperts and less educated people being systematically wrong about such matters.)

Even in cases where college professors are right that they are better at knowing, they need to be able to provide a better account of what makes them so: one that could earn the trust of those who inhabit different kinds of trust networks. In a world where people's informational trust networks diverge widely, the lack of such an account makes it hard to ease people's concerns about what college does to them or their children. Imagine, for instance, that I had told my conservative student and his father that the work we were doing in my class was meant to make the student a better knower and thinker, and then had backed that up by saying, either explicitly or in effect, that I was trying to make him think more like me. It is hard to imagine that this would have calmed their fears. After all, that is precisely what they came in to complain about!

In this chapter, I propose a way forward. It starts by turning the basic question around. Instead of asking what makes someone better at knowing, we can ask what makes someone worse at knowing. It turns out that there are some relatively clear ways an informational trust network can be dysfunctional as a basis for knowing. These have to do with its basic structure, rather than any particular feature of its content or informational ideology. By asking how to overcome such dysfunctional cognitive structures, we can piece together some of the work colleges do or might do as serving the aim of making students better at knowing. As the pieces come together, a new kind of informational trust network will emerge, one that I call a nondogmatic or open-minded network. Though this network resembles a broadly scientific network in certain aspects, it differs from it in ways that offer solutions to the problems uncovered in the previous chapters.

Dysfunctional Cognitive Structures and Their Repair

The most straightforward way a trust network can be dysfunctional as a means of knowing and understanding the world is if it has no way of considering and evaluating information from certain sources or kinds of sources, and thus no way of being challenged or corrected or improved by them and the potential information they provide. A network is clearly dysfunctional if it is completely closed to sets of sources in ways that are unconnected to any assessment of their reliability. This suggests that networks improve as bases for knowing insofar as they are open to new potential sources. Seeing the work of certain aspects of a college education in terms of what it undoes—how it opens otherwise closed networks—begins to point toward ways that colleges could make the education they provide more trustworthy. Consider, then, some relatively common dysfunctional structures and how a college might (and many colleges do) target them.

Informational Valleys

Someone in an informational valley can't see beyond the local peaks that surround her because she lacks access to certain sources of information. Informational valleys limit where their inhabitants can find information. They also limit the grounds of criticism the sources their inhabitants can access must withstand. This removes one way valley dwellers have of testing the trustworthiness of the informational sources in their trust network. Since someone stuck in an informational valley cannot make use of information beyond it to know more about the world or as a source of challenge to what she thinks she knows, being in an informational valley is a cognitive limitation.

Informational valleys can take many forms. Information can be blocked or withheld by various sources of authority, as when books are banned and information censored, classified, or hidden. Informational valleys can also result when certain kinds of information have no way of reaching someone, or reaching them in a way that might lead them to consider it as information. Someone who has never left their small town or segregated neighborhood or learned about what life is like outside it inhabits an informational valley, as does someone who has only ever spent time among highly educated elites and regards them as the only reliable sources of information. Someone can also inhabit an informational valley if they lack the tools to access or understand certain sources of information. A person who can't read inhabits a particularly narrow valley that blocks his access to all information that can only be accessed through the written word. People who only speak one language inhabit a valley that blocks their access to information in other languages that is either not translated or translated in such a way that something important is lost. As these examples suggest, the creation of informational valleys depends not only on where a person stands or what they can do, but on the ways the wider society is organized. The monolingual speaker of Pashto inhabits a much narrower valley than the monolingual speaker of English, because much more information is available in English than in Pashto. The person who can't read widens her valley if she has access to audio versions of texts or a text-reading device.

Informational valleys can be more or less sealed off from outside sources. They don't have to be completely sealed off to generate dysfunction. Consider, for instance, the attention paid to the elite end of the higher education environment by the mainstream media and a great deal of highly visible research. One source of this narrowing of attention is that most of the people doing the research and doing the reporting are themselves products of such elite schools and either work at them or mostly interact with people who work at them or went to them. This valley created by professional and personal contacts is not hermetically sealed. The people in question also no doubt have some contact with people who spent time in community colleges or never went to college, but this does not reorient the sense they have about which institutions or issues count as representative. Even a porous valley can impair our thinking.

Informational valleys are perhaps the most familiar dysfunctional structures, and they are a common target of all forms of education. When college leaders talk about broadening the horizons of their students, and general education requirements mandate that students study about foreign cultures, learn new languages, or explore new disciplines, they are aiming to pull their students out of the informational valleys they inhabit. However, if colleges want to genuinely help students out of informational valleys, they need to be careful that they are not merely moving their students from one valley to another. The academic silos that divide the disciplines also create informational valleys to the extent that members of one field only talk to one another about their work and never interact professionally with their colleagues in other fields, or to the extent that the outputs of those disciplines are indecipherable to outsiders. So, in training students in a discipline, colleges need to ensure that the informational trust networks they help students inhabit are not also cutting them off from sources of information. It is hard to notice that you occupy an informational valley on your own, and harder to acknowledge that you are in such a valley the more education you have received.

Filter Bubbles

Filter bubbles[1] do the same work as informational valleys: restricting access to certain sources of information. They do that work differently, however, and this can make them even harder to diagnose and repair. The key feature of a filter bubble is that it disguises the restrictions it places on information. Someone at the bottom of an informational valley might very well be aware that their horizons are limited. They may not care or think it hampers their ability to know what matters to them, and this will raise different problems. But assuming that is not the case, helping someone out of a valley is relatively straightforward: you teach them to access new kinds of information. Someone caught in a filter bubble, in contrast, is likely to think that they have access to all the information available. Consider, for instance, the filter bubble created by a newspaper of record, like the *New York Times*. It claims to give its readers "all the news that's fit to print," and suggests therein that it thus gives them all the news that genuinely matters. Like any paper, however, it makes choices about what to cover and what to print (because not all the news fits). Someone who learns about what is going on in the wider world only by reading the *Times* learns about only those parts of the world the paper pays attention to and reports on. Since its choices about what to cover are generally not themselves part of its reporting, someone who read every word in the paper every day but had no other sources of information still wouldn't be able to discern what information she had access to and what information she didn't. She would be in the equivalent of an informational valley but would be likely to think she was standing on a mountaintop with a broad and wide vista.

Note that the effect here is different from the one discussed above, where the reporters from the *Times* occupy an informational valley composed of products of elite higher education. Here the dysfunctional structure is that of the reader, who may not see as clearly the valleys her sources of information occupy. Consider, then, a reader who, for instance, gets all or almost all her information about higher education by reading the *New York Times*. Since it pays disproportionate attention to elite institutions without signaling that fact, it directs her attention to that limited sector as if it were the whole of higher education. That, in turn, shapes how she thinks about issues that arise in higher education. If, for instance, elite campuses are regularly embroiled in controversies over conservative student speech or the cancelation of provocative speakers' appearances on campus, and these are the sorts of items that get regularly reported in the *Times*, she is likely to infer that this is an issue that affects higher education generally. She may not notice or include in her thinking about speech on campus speech-related issues that have little to do with politics, like those that stem from the economic precarity of working-class students attending underfunded community colleges. If she is concerned about the effects of higher education on economic inequality, she may end up thinking only about policies that would open up elite admissions or offset the tuition burdens that come with attending elite schools. She may thereby miss the disparity in funding or subsidies available to students who attend different kinds of schools, or the ways that for most students facing economic hardship it is not tuition but the combination of other fees and the opportunity cost of lost family income that creates a financial obstacle to college attendance and completion.[2] Her thinking about these issues is rendered less good than it might have been if she had access to the information the *Times* filters out, or even if she were aware that her primary source of information is serving as a filter. The filter bubble she inhabits can affect her thinking this way even if it is somewhat porous. That is, even if she occasionally encounters information about non-elite schools, whether in her regular news source or elsewhere, it might be insufficient to shift where she directs her attention when she thinks about this question.

As a result of electronic communication and the accessibility of vast amounts of information via the internet, many of us have replaced our informational valleys with filter bubbles. In theory, we have access to much more information than we can possibly handle, process, or attend to, and from a much wider variety of sources. We make that huge quantity of information manageable by relying on various tools that filter out huge swaths of it. In general, we don't know much about the features of the filters we employ. We interact with search engines and news amalgamators as if they give us unmediated access to the vast digital world. But this isn't the case. Search results on Google or the contents of Facebook feeds, for instance, are a function of the information they have amassed on users and those who are paying them for access to those users. These results do not provide unfiltered, direct access to what is available on the internet about a given topic. Newspapers and news networks are also driven in what they report by the economic imperative of garnering the attention of viewers and readers and delivering that attention to their advertisers.[3] Moreover, Google and Facebook's filters reinforce sources of information we have relied on in the past and thereby further fortify and insulate our bubbles. The problem with filter bubbles is not merely that they limit the information we take in and think with. Such limitations are inevitable; we are limited creatures with limited cognitive capacities. The problem arises when we don't also have access to their procedures and algorithms for filtering, when we have no way of scrutinizing them or considering the sorts of challenges that might thus come from the information they filter out.

A college can help its students develop tools and dispositions to notice and scrutinize the filter bubbles they inhabit through classes in critical thinking, media literacy, and the sociology of knowledge production that are designed for this purpose. It could also help students escape from or at least move among different filter bubbles by giving students the skills to engage with and use a wide variety of potential information sources—by, for instance, learning the broad array of evidentiary practices found among academic disciplines as well as ways of engaging with the world not institutionalized in the academy. As the examples of the *New York Times* and search engines were meant to make clear, filter bubbles are not merely a trap for the less educated. And so, as with the aim of helping students out of informational valleys, a college that aims to help its students escape the filter bubbles that render their thinking less functional also has to pay attention to whether or not it is merely replacing one set of filters with another, different set.

Echo Chambers and Social Nests

Echo chambers, like informational valleys and filter bubbles, block the possibility of having one's beliefs challenged from certain directions, and this is the source of their dysfunction. But unlike valleys and bubbles, echo chambers work by shaping their inhabitants' evaluations of the trustworthiness of sources rather than their access to those sources. Someone stuck in an echo chamber not only receives heavy doses of mutually reinforcing information but is primed to distrust sources from outside the chamber. Cults and conspiracy theories sustain themselves by creating and maintaining echo chambers, and some scholars argue that right-wing media in the US does so as well.[4] Correcting the effects of an echo chamber requires more than exposure to new sources of information. Someone who is stuck in an echo chamber often regards the presentation of new information from a new source that challenges her views as an attempt to manipulate her. Her response to such information is not to question her original beliefs, but to strengthen her conviction in them as a defensive measure against manipulation. As a result, standard educational pathways can have difficulty breaking down echo chambers.

What often does work to help people escape echo chambers, though, is to change their social networks. Someone in an echo chamber who comes to befriend a person outside it (perhaps because they have been assigned to room together or work together as lab partners) can develop reasons to trust that person as a friend. When that friend then challenges or merely questions beliefs or sources that are current inside the echo chamber, the person in the echo chamber may be more receptive to that challenge. Colleges can thus help their students overcome this form of structural dysfunction by creating an environment where people can foster close social ties across the boundaries of their echo chambers, whether with their lab partners, roommates, teachers, advisors, or classmates.[5]

Like echo chambers, social nests lead their inhabitants to regard outside sources as less trustworthy than sources within the network. The difference is that a social nest increases trust levels within the network rather than priming distrust of sources outside it. Members of a close-knit community with strong social ties can build a social nest for themselves if being tied to the community is made easier by sharing its trust network. Agreeing with your friends and neighbors about which sources are trustworthy and why facilitates easy communication and social bonding. If that connection is seen as a good, then there is reason to trust those sources more thoroughly, even in the face of challenges to them. Not every close-knit community forms an echo chamber or a social nest. Part of what makes these structures dysfunctional is their extreme nature. Merely being wary of outsiders or having outlooks in common with a group of people does not place one in an echo chamber or social nest.

Since social nests provide a social value for their inhabitants, pulling someone out of a social nest can impose social costs on them. Many of the social costs canvassed in chapter 4 can be seen as the result of colleges pulling students out of various social nests. This means that a college education that serves to help students out of social nests will have to do so with care on two fronts: it will be important to build a trust network for students that does not cut them off from the social nests they previously inhabited, and it will be important not to bring them out of one social nest or echo chamber only to enfold them in a different one. A relatively closed-off and sufficiently self-satisfied educated class can form an echo chamber or a social nest just as effectively as an alienated, marginalized, or resentful one can.

The structures discussed here do not, by any means, exhaust the forms of structural dysfunction to be found in our cognitive architectures.[6] But they provide one path for constructing a genuinely trustworthy informational trust network. The various cognitive structures discussed above fail because they close off certain avenues of challenge and criticism, whether by limiting their inhabitants' access to certain kinds of information or by leading them to dismiss that information. That suggests that we can build more functional cognitive structures—better informational trust networks—by making openness to challenge a main criterion of trustworthiness. A network built on such a foundation would be made up of sources which, whatever their means of generating, discovering, and transmitting information, remained always open to being challenged or criticized. Someone who inhabited such a network would see dogmatism—the unwillingness or inability to countenance certain lines of criticism—as a sign of untrustworthiness. They would take open-mindedness as a reason to trust.

From Broadly Scientific Thinking to Open-Mindedness

Colleges could better respond to critics and those they speak for while also improving their students as knowers if the education they provided built an open-minded informational trust network for students instead of a broadly scientific one. The difference between broadly scientific and open-minded networks is subtle, and they are often taken to be the same thing. They differ most fundamentally in the ideology on which each one rests. A broadly scientific trust network evaluates the trustworthiness of sources based on whether they rely on broadly scientific methods of discovery and investigation. In contrast, an open-minded network evaluates sources for trustworthiness by looking at whether they remain always open to all sorts of challenges and criticism, even those that come from sources that do not rely on broadly scientific methods. The difference between them turns on a distinction between being rational and being nondogmatic.[7] A stretch of thinking is rational if it follows the rules and canons of rationality. These include the laws of logic, but also the norms and principles that set out what counts as evidence for what. Connected to these rules is a view about objectivity and generality that plays a big role in broadly scientific trust networks: general results are taken to be more objective than highly localized ones, and methods that have general application are taken to be more objective than those rooted in highly situated, local experience. Conclusions based on wide and representative data sets are thus favored over those based on a single anecdote, even one that is richly described, and the results of random-controlled trials are favored over judgments that stem from the sort of inarticulable expert sensibility derived from long experience. Rationality-based informational ideologies also generally draw a sharp distinction between facts and values, and so regard as confused any criteria for determining the trustworthiness of a source of information that point to its moral qualities or its role in benefiting or harming certain people or populations. A rationality-based informational ideology grounds its evaluation of the trustworthiness of sources on the rationality of their forms of thinking and methods of discovery. This is precisely the sort of structure exhibited by the broadly scientific trust network that I have argued colleges tend to build for their students.

In contrast, a stretch of thinking is nondogmatic if it remains always open to challenge. Someone who holds their positions nondogmatically allows that there might be reasons to reject or alter them and that they should be on the lookout for challenges to or criticisms of the position they hold, including from unfamiliar places or expressed in unfamiliar idioms. An informational ideology that is grounded in nondogmatism evaluates the trustworthiness of sources of information not directly, by looking at the methods used to arrive at their conclusions, but indirectly, based on whether the conclusion is held open to challenge and has so far withstood any challenges raised. It regards any form of close-mindedness and dogmatism, even dogmatic adherence to the methods of science, as a reason to withhold or reduce trust in a given source of information.

Many sources that use broadly scientific methods to generate or verify information are also nondogmatic, and so will figure in an open-minded network as well. The key difference is that inhabiting an open-minded network requires being open to nonscientifically grounded challenges as well. In fact, one important feature of sources that pass muster and thus comprise an open-minded network is that they can rely on a wider variety of methods (including those that are typical of nonscientific trust networks). Inhabiting an open-minded trust network involves being open to the sources that make up and the people who inhabit all sorts of trust networks. This makes it possible to inhabit an open-minded trust network in a way that doesn't wholly reject these other trust networks, even those that are not compatible with broadly scientific networks. At the same time, inhabiting an open-minded trust network does not involve rejecting or abandoning a commitment to reason; it is merely a matter of understanding differently what that commitment entails.

Since those who inhabit an open-minded trust network must consider challenges from all kinds of sources, coming to inhabit an open-minded network does not require rejecting the sources you previously trusted. In fact, it is helped by a familiarity with their terms of and criteria for judgment insofar as these can be sources of challenge and criticism as one encounters a variety of new sources and the information they provide.

A college that helped its students build and inhabit open-minded trust networks would improve them as knowers, even in comparison with those who inhabit a broadly scientific network. Dysfunctional cognitive structures are rendered dysfunctional by their inability to take on board or take seriously certain types of information. Coming to inhabit an open-minded network combats that source of dysfunction. To be able to take challenges seriously and ascertain whether sources of information do so as well, students have to learn to understand and appreciate the force of such challenges. Moreover, they need to develop better evaluative skills: being open to challenge means considering challenges, not automatically accepting them. Students only effectively remain open to challenge if they can think well about the force of those challenges and evaluate them in ways that withstand further criticism. This combination of improvements protects them from various sorts of blindness and myopia that can result from occupying other kinds of trust networks, including networks that are broadly scientific. Both the farmer who outright rejects scientific advice about how to improve his crop yields or his own health and the USDA agent who makes those recommendations without accounting for the knowledge of local variations the farmer has accumulated over many years are blinded by their trust networks. Each would think better about farming if they entertained seriously the challenge of the other.

Beyond making students better knowers, helping students to build and inhabit truly open-minded trust networks would balance out the social costs imposed by a college education. On the one hand, it would require that even those students who grew up among people with college educations and thus inhabit broadly scientific networks learn to inhabit a different trust network than their parents and home communities. More importantly, they would have to learn to be more open to the voices and perspectives of other sectors of society and less confident in the unimpeachability of the trust network they grew up inhabiting. On the other hand, it would lessen the strain on social networks that the development of a new informational trust network can cause. This is because an open-minded trust network does not reject input from those who inhabit other trust networks. Someone who inhabited an open-minded network will thus not find it as hard to remain in easy conversation with those with whom they grew up who continue to occupy different networks. Though their networks no longer coincide, they still overlap, and that makes the process of maintaining social ties easier to manage.

The student who begins college inhabiting a highly local and situated trust network may find in it resources to raise important challenges to certain results produced by the broadly scientific methods she learns about in a class. A teacher who aims to teach her how to inhabit an open-minded network while teaching her the methods of a particular science can recognize that the knowledge she arrives with and the trust networks that support it give her material to work with as she builds out this new network. He need not view his job as helping her build a radically new worldview, of plucking her off her cognitive island and bringing her onto his. He can merely help her to expand the trust network she grew up inhabiting, so she can build bridges between the various islands.

Of course, shifting from the local network to the open-minded one changes the trust network she inhabits, and this may still have profound transformative effects on her. She learns to value characteristics like humility, a willingness to be challenged, and the kind of mental flexibility necessary to appreciate challenges from perhaps unfamiliar places in unfamiliar idioms, rather than embeddedness in a local context, as signs of trustworthiness. She can, nevertheless, learn to value such traits without completely dismissing the grounds for trust she has previously relied on and which are common among her community back home. That can reduce the social strains her education creates and make it easier for her to maintain her social ties.[8]

Being more deliberate and self-conscious about helping students build open-minded trust networks could then shape several things colleges do, including what and how they teach. It could, for instance, open the door to entertaining and teaching nonscientific ways of thinking and knowing. It could also change how various broadly scientific methods of inquiry are taught. In the rest of this chapter, I offer some suggestions of what this might look like at the pedagogical and curricular levels. Some of these suggestions involve reinterpreting or articulating differently what colleges already do, and others involve changing at least some of what some colleges do. Some involve changes in institutional policy, structure, or curriculum, and others involve changes in how an individual instructor might teach her class or interact with her students. Some of them are being done already, at least in some places, and some of them would be easy to adopt, even if all of them, like any policies, have opportunity costs and involve trade-offs. None of them are likely to be applicable everywhere across the wide and heterogenous scope of US higher education, but hopefully they offer a range of ideas with which to begin thinking.

1. Teach "Charitable" Thinking

Colleges aim to teach students to be critical thinkers. They teach them how to dismantle bad arguments and evaluate and reject certain kinds of sources. So understood, critical thinking is a more or less negative process. Critical thinkers have and know how and when to use the skills to figure out why arguments, beliefs, and positions are wrong. As we saw in chapter 3, learning these skills tends to prune someone's informational trust network. In many college settings, these skills are also taught as a tool for developing or perfecting a broadly scientific informational ideology. Students learn, for instance, that randomized controlled trials and peer-reviewed sources are trustworthy, while general conclusions based on anecdotes are not. They learn that it is a mistake to treat someone's value orientation as a reason to trust them as a source of information.

In contrast, learning to think charitably can open up a person's trust network. Someone who thinks charitably about what they hear or read tries to figure out how someone who is smart, careful, thoughtful, and sincerely concerned with finding the correct answer could hold that view or come to that conclusion.[9] It is a way of taking what other people say seriously. Because open-mindedness requires being fully open to challenges from wherever they arise, it requires the skills of charitable thinking.

Several things make charitable thinking difficult. It can be emotionally taxing to entertain seriously challenges to and criticisms of our views—the thought that we are wrong about something. It is often easier and more comfortable to find ways to dismiss such challenges. That creates a temptation to adopt a distorted picture of what moves or informs our critics so that we can dismiss their challenge or refute it more easily. Sometimes we do this by making assumptions that they are like us in all important ways: that they must have the same aims, interests, and values we do, and thus that their coming to a different conclusion has to be a result of a mistake, rather than a genuinely different orientation. All these temptations to not think charitably are magnified when a challenge is made in terms that are unfamiliar, when it threatens positions we hold dear, or which protect things we value and about which we feel vulnerable. These temptations may be just as hard to overcome for those who inhabit a broadly scientific network as they are for those who don't. Broadly scientific networks can be dogmatically inhabited just as firmly as nonscientific networks.

Moreover, to really understand and appreciate how an unfamiliar position can provide insights worth taking seriously, we need a set of intellectual skills. Sometimes, a critic works from within a different cultural or disciplinary framework or intellectual tradition. If we want to understand their point, we need to understand where they are coming from, how they are using certain terms, and the background beliefs and values that are informing their position. It may require that we at least temporarily or imaginatively inhabit their perspective to be able to see why things look differently to them and whether, were we in their shoes, it would look differently to us.

Colleges who want to develop the skills of charitable thinking could do so by including courses that emphasize charitable thinking in their general education requirements or by pushing instructors to adopt the development of charitable as well as critical thinking among their learning goals. Instructors can help students develop these skills by modeling them and being explicit about how they are working to be charitable in their approach to questions, challenges, or positions they ultimately disagree with. Classes in critical thinking often ask students to evaluate claims and arguments made in popular fora and give them tools to criticize such arguments. A class that wanted to develop charitable thinking could ask students to engage in a kind of reverse activity: it could present students with positions the instructor expects them to find unfamiliar and difficult and then teach them to see what might be valuable there. A class whose students are overwhelmingly white might explore critical race theory. A class whose students are overwhelmingly progressive in their political outlook might explore conservative thought. By exposing students to a position they are likely to dismiss and find unfamiliar and uncomfortable, and helping them to treat it seriously, such courses can give students practice treating positions they disagree with charitably. In both cases, the idea would be neither to present these admittedly partisan intellectual traditions as one amongst a set of options for thinking about a problem, nor to convince students to adopt the positions they originally rejected. It would be to practice and develop skills in charitable thinking by learning to appreciate the force of an unfamiliar position. Since teaching students to think charitably about such traditions involves bringing out what is insightful and interesting about them, it is easily confused with teaching them for partisan purposes. Teachers who aim to teach charitable thinking through this approach thus need to be clear about what they are doing, and campus leaders must be able to articulate this difference to parents, communities, or oversight agencies that conflate the two.

Students can more easily overcome the emotional challenge of charitable thinking in spaces that are intellectually safe for them. Seriously considering a challenge to our views requires being vulnerable. If the view in question is one that we value, that informs our sense of who we are, or that supports our ties to particular communities, vulnerability may not be something we are willing to accept. A deeply secular student may have trouble taking seriously challenges to his positions that come from a religious perspective. A progressive student may find conservative challenges difficult to entertain seriously because she values her self-image as progressive and wants to protect it, or because she is concerned that genuinely engaging with the conservative critic will open the door to harms against her or those to whom she wants to be an ally. An intellectually safe environment is one where students can more readily accept that vulnerability, because they can trust that even if they face difficult challenges, they will be protected from harm and cared for. Note that this does not mean an environment where students are not challenged. Safety is, to the contrary, the condition which makes it possible for students to be challenged and to seriously take up those challenges. A classroom or other space where students exchange ideas can be made safe for them in several ways. Teachers can attempt to insulate students' social status outside of class from what they say in class. Teachers can emphasize that classroom discussions are made for trying thoughts out, for playing with ideas. This requires not only careful management on the part of teachers, but also a willingness on the part of students to view classroom discussions as somewhat insulated from the rest of life. At the same time, students should also think about their responsibility to make such spaces possible by not taking advantage of this freedom to try out potentially controversial or divisive ideas to deliberately target other students or make them feel uncomfortable. Balancing these concerns is difficult, and it requires guidance and practice. No social space can be completely walled off from others. No form of freedom isn't liable to abuse. But if we want students to develop the abilities to genuinely be open to and engage with challenges to what they think, it is work worth doing and a risk worth taking. Classrooms and other spaces are also made safer when students know that if they suffer harms there, they can count on being cared for. Teachers should thus also be prepared to support students who may bear extra costs of difficult engagements or who end up being hurt or harmed by what happens in a classroom, and they should make it clear to students ahead of time that they will be there in that role.

Someone who approaches unfamiliar ideas, arguments, and sources of information charitably does not merely accept them or treat them as if they cannot be subject to evaluation. Inhabiting an open-minded trust network does not amount to accepting relativism—the view that there is no way to judge or evaluate positions that work within a different cultural frame, or that all ways of thinking about something are equally good. As we will see below, open-mindedness also requires good evaluative skills.

2. Teach Flexible Thinking

To inhabit an open-minded trust network, students also need to learn how to move amongst intellectual perspectives and think about a topic from points of view that might raise challenges to their current positions. Colleges that aim to build open-minded networks for their students thus need to teach their students the skills of flexible thinking as well. The flexible thinker can move adroitly among perspectives and points of view to see how a question or issue looks from within different cultural or intellectual traditions. Most importantly, a flexible thinker can entertain a variety of grounds for trust and distrust of sources of information. She can appreciate what the informational landscape looks like from within a variety of trust networks. This flexibility helps avoid various forms of inadvertent close-mindedness brought on by an inability to appreciate alternative approaches to a question.

One way to develop flexibility of thought is through deep exposure to a variety of different positions, perspectives, traditions, and trust networks. A college's general education programs are thus a natural place to teach these skills, but to do this work such programs need to be designed and curated with that end in mind. First, a general education program would have to expose students to a variety of ways of thinking along a variety of dimensions: a variety not only of academic disciplines, but also of broad intellectual traditions and cultural orientations, all chosen to expose the student to a varied set of kinds of trust networks. While this might be accomplished by a student taking a couple of courses in each of the humanities, social sciences, and natural sciences, or courses fitted into broad content categories, it won't happen merely through such requirements. A more deliberate curation of the courses any individual student takes to satisfy general education requirements would be necessary to create variety on all these dimensions.

Moreover, not every class in a field, and not all subject matter in which a particular approach or perspective is taken, will contribute to the cultivation of flexible thinkers. Classes designed as the first course in a major should try to help students begin to fully inhabit the ways of thinking particular to that discipline. An introduction to sociology designed for potential majors should start to teach students how to think like sociologists. Courses whose purpose in the curriculum is to help students develop into flexible thinkers may need to be taught and organized differently. A sociology course designed for a general education curriculum aimed at developing flexible thinkers might be designed to make clear how thinking like a sociologist is different from thinking like an economist or historian, or it might be designed to teach students how to imaginatively inhabit the trust networks laid out in a set of sociological studies without spending time on the specific methods sociologists use to do their research. When colleges populate their general education requirements with lists of basic departmental introductory courses, they can miss the opportunity to teach flexible thinking through those requirements.

Even when students take a set of courses each designed to teach a distinctive way of thinking, they may fail to develop intellectual flexibility. Consider a student who wanders through distributional requirements that teach her to think in different ways, but teach each way of thinking as specific to a different topic. She might learn to think like or about taxi drivers in Mumbai using one set of techniques, the effects of climate change on temperate rainforests with a different set of techniques, and the workings of the US education system with a third set. She may fail to see how these techniques and modes of thought might all be directed to the same phenomenon or to learn how to move between them. Colleges that want to foster skills of flexible thinking could avoid this result by offering sets of courses that look at the same set of phenomena from a variety of perspectives, or by offering courses that include a variety of disciplinary approaches to the same topic. They could then build their general education requirements around such course clusters. Imagine a series of classes on forests, for instance: one that approaches forests as biological ecosystems, another that examines them from the perspective of various forest-dwelling communities and cultures, a third that treats them as economic resources, and another that looks at their role in moderating planetary systems that affect climate. A student who took all four classes would be more likely to appreciate how to move among perspectives in order to understand something than if she were exposed to these ways of thinking about different topics. A college that developed specific pathways like this for satisfying general education requirements designed to expose students to taking different perspectives on a single topic would help their students develop the skills and habits of flexible thinking.

3. Equip Students to Engage With and Evaluate Challenges

Someone who is open to challenges does not merely accept all of them. Sometimes a belief is correct or a value judgment appropriate, and it can and should withstand the challenges raised to it. People who inhabit an open-minded network don't just take seriously new and challenging positions. They also have the tools to critically evaluate the challenges and criticisms they take seriously. Even when colleges are teaching students positions about which there is wide and broad consensus or which are generally considered as settled, they can help build evaluative skills. While this can sometimes be done by explicitly considering challenges to those positions with students in the classroom, that is not required. Consider, for instance, a class in evolutionary biology. A class could produce open-minded biologists without teaching alternative explanations for the diversity and structure of living things. It would not need to teach or entertain and refute intelligent design, for instance. But a professor who taught evolutionary biology with the aim of helping her students build and inhabit an open-minded informational trust network might think of her learning objectives in terms of what adequate and genuine engagement with an advocate of intelligent design would involve. She might take as a criterion of whether she has successfully taught her students evolutionary biology that they would be able to engage with someone who challenged their views from a perspective that accepted intelligent design and rebut that challenge without merely dismissing it. That might involve spending more time on the evidentiary basis of claims about evolution generally, or on what it is trying to explain and what it isn't trying to explain. It need not require introducing her students to intelligent design, giving it equal time, or even devoting time to refuting it. The aim would be to make sure that her students' knowledge of evolutionary biology was not dogmatically held, even while making sure it was securely and firmly held.

The difference between teaching students the skills necessary to evaluate challenges within an open-minded network and within a broadly scientific network comes to this: within a broadly scientific network, challenges can be rejected for not being sufficiently scientific or based in the forms and methods a broadly scientific trust network takes as criteria of trustworthiness. Within an open-minded network, it is not enough to reject challenges because they do not adhere to broadly scientific criteria for trustworthiness. Rather, the inhabitants of such a network think more charitably about what the criticism is bringing up and why, and look for ways of responding that don't just assume that they already occupy the only perspective from which the question can be legitimately approached or answered.

4. Cultivate Intellectual Humility

Those who can combine the skills of charitable and flexible thinking with a capacity to nevertheless evaluate claims, criticisms, and points of view possess the virtue of intellectual humility. Intellectually humble people are open to the thought that they might be wrong about what they think or believe or claim to know. They are, as Kyla Ebels-Duggan puts it, "slow to attribute disagreement to intellectual laziness, stupidity, or moral turpitude on the part of their interlocutors," and they "recognize the genuine difficulty of serious intellectual tasks."[10] It isn't that they never reach a decision or form a belief. Rather, they are prepared and willing to reevaluate what they have decided or believe in the face of challenges, new information, or new ways of making sense of the world. Intellectually humble people are always ready to learn and to think again, in large part because they are aware of their own cognitive limitations in the face of genuinely difficult problems.

Intellectual humility requires avoiding both radical skepticism and relativism. Radical skeptics think we can never really know anything, so they can appear to be models of intellectual humility. They start, however, from a final and unchallengeable stance: that the world is essentially unknowable by the human mind. While radical skepticism provides a standpoint from which to reject various forms of dogmatism, it is itself a form of dogmatism that fails to take seriously the possibility of challenges from non-skeptical positions.

Relativists, on the other hand, hold that everyone's positions or values are equally valid, and also often claim that everything (or at least all value) is graspable only from within a particular person's subjective perspective. Relativists think that people can never know the world in the way others do, and that since all claims about the world are subjective in this way, each is as good as any other. Relativism can thus seem to be the position from which charitable thinking grows, and a form of intellectual humility and open-mindedness, since it refuses to stand in judgment over other people's beliefs or value judgments. But relativists, like skeptics, begin from a premise they do not leave open to challenge. They thus reject intellectual humility.

Colleges that teach students to recognize and value intellectual humility in others and cultivate it in themselves help them to build and inhabit open-minded trust networks. Colleges can help foster intellectual humility through the design of their curricula as well as in their pedagogy. One path to intellectual humility is exposure to genuinely hard problems: problems for which we do not already know the answers or the methods that might uncover them. Colleges can require students to take courses that expose them to such problems and that show them how prevalent such problems are. Philosophy classes are particularly good for this task, as philosophers make a habit of taking the seemingly obvious and showing it to be more complicated and difficult. (It is, of course, not the only discipline in which this can be done.)

Exposure to genuinely difficult problems will foster intellectual humility only if teachers also help students appreciate that sustained, careful, flexible, and collaborative work can nevertheless hope to make progress on such problems. One way to do that is to show students how, for many issues widely regarded as settled, a great deal of work went into finding a solution or generating a solid scientific or social consensus. A commitment to human equality and the dignity of each person, the view that many human diseases are caused by viruses and bacteria, the second law of thermodynamics, and the calculus are all monumental human achievements that are generally taught as basic facts, principles, and methods. But they could, instead, be taught in ways that bring out how very smart and thoughtful people once got them wrong and how consensus on them was changed. Students can thus be brought to appreciate just how hard certain kinds of problems can be, and at the same time see that concerted effort can make progress toward solving them, even if that progress is not linear. They can come to appreciate that those who have made the most progress toward solutions are often the most humble about what they have actually achieved, because they see more clearly than others just how hard the issues are and how much further there is to go.

Teachers can better foster intellectual humility if they also model it: striving to be open to their students' challenges and criticisms. Being open to students' challenges has the added benefit of showing students that the challenges they are moved to raise to what they are being taught are worth taking seriously, even when they are ultimately rejected. It helps students recognize that a community of intellectually humble people who nevertheless possess great expertise can be welcoming to and accommodating of newcomers.

5. Get Students to Figure Things Out Together

A further advantage of exposing students to genuinely hard problems is that it gives them an experience in which open-mindedness and its associated skills—charitable and flexible thinking alongside evaluative capacities—is clearly useful. Seeing that there are problems whose solution requires the pooling of many perspectives and approaches helps students see the value of developing these skills. In like manner, giving them smaller problems to solve that have these features can give them practice in using these skills. Problem-solving exercises and problem sets are familiar features of classes in math, the natural sciences, and the more quantitative social sciences like economics. They tend to be absent from classes in the humanities and the qualitative social sciences. Students in a literature or ethics class are not likely to be asked to do problem sets. Instead, they may be expected to discuss readings or debate controversial topics. They may be asked to write essays that express and defend a point of view. This pedagogical difference rests on and reinforces a common perception of the central difference between these fields. It is common for students to think of math and the natural sciences as fields in which there are determinate answers to questions, and that learning the subject is in large part learning the techniques for finding such answers. In contrast, they think that the topics pondered in the humanities are questions for which there are no right answers, so everyone is entitled to their own beliefs (perhaps only as long as they can properly defend them).

This common perception misrepresents how practitioners think about their own research in both kinds of fields, however, and it leads students away from the kind of work that might confront them with the sort of hard problems best approached through an open-minded trust network. Researchers and scholars across the university might describe their own research as trying to figure something out: how a complex causal process or social dynamic works, what relationship obtains between different ideas or abstract structures, or how to achieve certain ends given certain tools and under certain constraints. What they are trying to figure out may not yet be amenable to an easily applied method. They thus spend time discussing how to think about it and from what perspective they might find illumination. They are constrained in their attempts to think about it by what generates insight. Not every idea they encounter or consider will be a good one. Research across the university thus partakes of both of the kinds of activities that traditional modes of instruction separate—solving problems and discussion. Moreover, much research is motivated by a set of thoughts about its target that students can find hard to see as mutually compatible: (1) the question I am thinking about has a correct answer, (2) we can make progress toward answering it if we start from the assumption that it has a correct answer, despite the fact that (3) no one (yet) knows what that answer is, and 4) perhaps no one knows for sure how to find the correct answer or how we would be sure we had found it if we did.

Students tend to think that if the first and second are true, the third and fourth cannot be, and vice versa. This attitude is reinforced when they encounter only problem-set-based pedagogy in math and the natural sciences and only discussion-based pedagogy in the humanities. If students think that problems with answers can be solved straightforwardly and questions that can't be so solved have no answers, then they won't see that there are hard problems of the sort that both require and help foster intellectual humility and open-mindedness.

One way, then, for faculty to challenge and change these attitudes is by broadening out their pedagogical techniques in all subjects to bring out the aspects of their field that are hidden from view by its traditional pedagogical approaches. Math and science classes can show a greater awareness of the methods of those fields as tools for plumbing areas of uncertainty rather than merely as algorithms for generating answers. Math and science classes that involve peer instruction or that task groups of students with working together to figure out how to solve genuinely hard problems (not merely those that require the application of a theory or formula just learned) can help students appreciate the value of pooling different points of view. Programs that include opportunities for genuine research can expose students in these fields to the sorts of uncertainties they may think only characterize the humanities.

Conversely, classes in the humanities can teach problem-solving techniques, and set students tasks that require such problem solving. This can avoid some of the standard pitfalls of humanities classes that include discussion. Consider two common forms of discussion found in many humanities classes: Some classroom discussion aims to clear up student confusions—a teacher stops her lecture and asks if her students have any questions. Other discussions aim to let students air their positions on an issue and perhaps, if they disagree with one another, debate the issue in question. The teacher asks them to discuss a proposition by asking them what they think about it. With the first move, students are implicitly taught that there is a settled right answer and once one knows it, there is no more to be said on the matter. With the second, students are taught that while people may disagree with one another, there is nothing more to be said beyond fighting it out, even if civilly and with words and reasons. In contrast, when students are asked to solve a difficult (for them) problem, their discussion can have a point: figuring out together a suitable method and implementing it. This may require considering various possibilities, and different students may approach the question from different perspectives. They will be most successful if they listen to one another and try to understand each other's ideas and how they are thinking about the problem. They thus learn to use the traits of mind necessary for inhabiting an open-minded trust network, because these are what leads them successfully to the goal that has been set for them.

Such problems can be large-scale questions for which even a whole semester is not enough, or more focused issues that can be worked out in part of a class period. For instance, an introductory political philosophy class could be oriented around trying to figure out whether the US is a genuine democracy. As the semester unfolds and students are tasked with reading and understanding various difficult texts, they could be asked to solve more limited problems: is this passage from Aristotle's *Politics* best understood as defining a term or making an empirical claim? What are the steps in this argument for restricting immigration? Alternatively, students can be given concrete cases or dilemmas that engage with the issues being taught in the class. Students are asked to figure out what to do or advise, or steps along the way to doing this, rather than to discuss or debate the more abstract issues a solution must navigate. Case-based instruction is, of course, a mainstay of much pre-professional education. I am suggesting here that it might also find an expanded role in courses in the liberal arts and sciences.[11] In the course of trying to solve problems or figure out what to do in a case, students may end up thinking about a number of controversial issues about which they no doubt have different opinions. Raising these issues within the activity of problem solving, however, incentivizes students to remain open to challenge rather than to harden their positions or conclude that all these different positions are merely a matter of opinion.

Teaching this way requires more explicitly teaching students how to work through the kinds of questions being posed and how to develop techniques for working together. If one of its aims is to help students build new trust networks that take seriously challenges to their habitual ways of thinking without merely teaching them that they must abandon those ways of thinking, then it may require careful curation, and its direction and emphases may depend to a large degree on the kinds of students found in a given classroom.

6. Model Openness in Teaching

Finally, if faculty members wish to help their students build and inhabit open-minded informational trust networks, they need to model what inhabiting such networks looks like. Faculty members model open-mindedness in their teaching when they avoid the poses and stances of intellectual arrogance and unimpeachable expertise and take seriously what students bring into classrooms and the challenges they raise to what their teachers say or have them read or do. Doing so can be a challenge. When trying to explain complex and unfamiliar material to students, it is often necessary to simplify it in various ways. Often the process of simplification involves ignoring hedges or aspects of uncertainty in a field's knowledge of something. In presenting some material in as simple and straightforward a way as possible, it is very easy to give off the impression that it is unimpeachably true, and that there is no way a thoughtful person could disagree. It can take extra work to both simplify the development of a field and yet model open-mindedness.

A different problem can emerge in more advanced classes. These aim to help students fully immerse themselves in and develop expertise in a certain discipline. These classes often encourage students to inhabit a trust network that, at least as it is being constructed, may be somewhat siloed. An upper-level biology class designed to help students develop fluency with a set of techniques or a set of theories in a limited time period may need to ignore philosophical or ethical questions, or even questions that come at the issue from the perspective of chemistry or physiology. It is easy for this to slip into a form of close-mindedness. Deliberate effort may be needed to avoid that.

Finally, in many college classrooms, faculty are teaching material about which they are particularly expert and about which they have rather stable and settled views, in part because they have already considered a wide range of challenges to the positions they hold. Some of the work that has gone into their forming those opinions depends on aspects of their expertise that their students don't yet share. Even if a faculty member wants to be open to rehearsing various challenges and responses to those challenges, it might not be possible to be fully transparent about that process with his students. It can be hard, when teaching such material, to teach it as if it is still an open question. Modeling open-mindedness in such a situation requires working against this difficulty.[12]

One way to begin this process is to abandon what pedagogy experts refer to as "sage on the stage" methods of teaching. It is harder to model open-mindedness when you are lecturing to students than when helping them work through an unfamiliar (even if only to them) problem (being "a guide on the side"). It can also be helpful for teachers to teach at least some material on which they don't have a settled view, or to apply it to problems they have not fully worked out yet. This will of course be harder in some fields and classes than others. At the very least, though, teachers can adopt this position when they are in the classroom. The issue here is not really whether or not to disclose their position on an issue.[13] It is the stance the teacher in an introductory math class takes when she asks her students to work on a problem and, when they get stuck, asks them to try out ways forward and see if they work rather than telling them what the next step is or giving them a recipe for solving problems like this.

A teacher who helps her students figure things out can also more easily model the stance she takes toward her research—that the problems she works on can have objective answers even if we don't know what they are or how to find them, and even when we are not sure whether we would know they were right if we did find them. By explicitly modeling open-mindedness in parts of her teaching, she can help her students appreciate why an open-minded outlook may sit behind even the most seemingly didactic of positions and explanations.

Colleges that build broadly scientific informational trust networks for their students who arrive on campus occupying different networks wind up taking them off one cognitive island only to place them on another, albeit one that is larger and provides access to more social advantages. This process imposes social costs on those students and on the communities they come from. In contrast, a college that helped its students build and inhabit open-minded trust networks would help those students become bridges between the trust networks inhabited by those they meet and learn from in college and the networks inhabited by people back home. Nevertheless, learning to inhabit an open-minded trust network still represents a profound change from inhabiting a more closed-off network, even one that is broadly scientific. The education envisaged in this chapter will still be transformative for many students, even if it doesn't fully alienate them from their families and home communities. Even colleges that cultivate open-mindedness will need their students to be open to being changed—to be vulnerable. Students and their parents and communities will only accept such vulnerability if they trust the colleges who expect it. Chapter 6 offers further pathways by which colleges might earn and be worthy of such trust.

{6}

What Colleges Could Do, Part 2

EARNING AND SUSTAINING TRUST

Colleges can earn and be worthy of the trust they require and ask for by taking action along three paths. First, they can show proper appreciation and gratitude for the trust placed in them. Being entrusted with a valuable or difficult task is a form of honor, and so showing gratitude for that honor demonstrates appreciation of the seriousness of that task.[1] Second, they can care not only for their students but for those students' families and communities. Being a trustworthy caretaker requires caring for not only what is entrusted to you, but also for those who bestow this responsibility. If a friend asks me to take care of his prized Ming vase while he is having work done in his house, it isn't enough that I protect the vase from harm. I also need to not act in ways that would increase his anxiety about the vase's safety. I shouldn't, for instance, juggle the vase even if, being an expert juggler, I am at no risk of dropping it. Doing so would fail to show proper concern for my friend. Colleges can show care for students and their families in part by not acting in ways that heighten their anxiety. Finally, colleges can respond with reciprocity by being open to being changed by their students. The point of such reciprocity is not to give those seeking an education counter leverage or a bargaining chip. It is, rather, meant to shift the inevitable power dynamics that come from putting oneself in the care of another. Reciprocally trusting those I want to trust me shifts us from a unidirectional relationship in which one party asks something of another, to a mutual relationship in which we engage in an activity together. Consider, then, what might be done along each of these paths.

7. Show Gratitude[2]

There are at least three sorts of actions that call for gratitude. First, a person or what they have to offer might be chosen from a range of available options. A company that thanks its customers in addition to providing them with the product or service they purchased is expressing gratitude for their choice. Since students generally have a choice of which college to attend, which courses to take, and which subjects to study, there is a role for this kind of gratitude in higher education. Second, a person might receive a gift. A true gift is not owed or deserved. Its recipient isn't entitled to it and owes nothing to the giver in return. And yet, an expression of gratitude—of recognition that a gift has been given when it was not owed—is an appropriate response. Students can make a gift of their attention, enthusiasm, and dedication when this rises above the level that is asked for or required by a class. Teachers can project their own humility by treating their students' enthusiastic engagement in their classes as a gift rather than their due and responding to it with gratitude. Finally, a person might bestow an honor or esteem. Although an honor can be deserved or merited, it is not something to which the honoree is entitled. It thus shares some, but not all, features with a gift. When students enroll in a given college or class, they do not merely choose them out of a range of options. Students also honor the college or the class's teacher in bestowing upon them a certain confidence in their ability to educate the students well. A student who signs up for (and stays in) one of my classes judges that what I can teach her is worthy of her time, effort, and tuition, as she has previously judged that my university is so worthy. That is a mark of esteem, and I can demonstrate that I not only recognize and value her esteem but will aim to be worthy of it by showing gratitude for it.

Showing gratitude in this third case can be as simple as explicitly saying "thank you" to my students—not for choosing my class or my college, but for entrusting me with part of their education. More generally, such gratitude can shape a college's interaction with students and the policies it adopts. It rules out, for instance, policies and practices that grow out of or express contempt and derision toward students or the social worlds from which they come. I can't be grateful to a student or a student's family for the trust placed in me and at the same time think my job is merely to cavalierly pull them apart from one another or rescue them from confusion and ignorance. It may be that my effect on my student will be to move her away from the influence of her family, and it may even be that this is one of the things she is trusting me to help her with. But taking on even that task with gratitude for the trust placed in me changes how I engage with the elements of the informational and social trust networks she currently inhabits. I need to be aware of the gravity of what I am being entrusted with and clear about its boundaries.

If, however, colleges want to be fully worthy of the trust placed in them, they need to not only express gratitude for that trust and cultivate the attitude the gratitude expresses, but also act in ways that are fully worthy of that trust: they need to show care for those who are entrusted to them even as they work to change them.

8. Take Care

Failing to care for that which is entrusted to you betrays that trust. In addition to ethical reasons for not betraying students' trust, there are pragmatic reasons as well: colleges will have a much harder time effectively educating students who do not trust them. Students, their families, and their communities entrust colleges with the student's education. Colleges educate students by refurbishing their informational trust networks and their criteria for judging the trustworthiness of sources. Colleges are not trusted under that description, but caring for what is entrusted to them nevertheless involves caring not only for their students, but also for those students' relationships to their current trust networks.

Caring in this way has several elements. First, colleges should take care that they do this work well. That means making sure that the informational trust networks they help their students inhabit are in fact improvements over those the students start with. College faculty and administrators can become complacent in the superiority of their forms of thought and the routes they take to acquire knowledge. They can become overly confident that their own trust networks are not plagued by the dysfunctional structures they work to help their students escape. Caring for their students requires that they remain attentive to the possibility that their own networks are not above reproach. Faculty members should be continually on guard against the ways a collective practice of like-minded and similarly trained experts can become close-minded both as they pursue their own research and as they teach. This, of course, is part of remaining open-minded, but it is worth remembering the sorts of pressures a discipline or department can exert against such open-mindedness and striving to overcome or reduce them.

Second, teachers should be thoughtful and intentional about the sort of informational trust networks they want their students to build and inhabit. They should not assume that the trust networks that would make their students better knowers are going to be exactly the same as those which make them (the teachers) better researchers. Some of the narrow norms and practices of an academic discipline are designed to push the boundaries of specialized knowledge. They may not be as desirable in the informational trust network of someone who is merely majoring in a field. Thinking of the undergraduate curriculum as building broadly trustworthy trust networks for students affects how it should be designed. Several years ago, my department considered making revisions to its undergraduate major. One of my colleagues asked us each to consider what kind of training we would want an incoming PhD student to have when they arrived. We all treated that framing as more or less obviously right. I now think that was a mistake. We might have better served our students by asking what sorts of benefits the sustained study of philosophy can hope to bring to someone's informational trust network and more generally to their capacities to know and think. From there, we could have thought about what sort of coursework would make it most likely that our students would reap those benefits by studying with us. We would have left to the side the further question of whether these were also the capacities needed to succeed in a PhD program or as a philosophy professor.

Third, colleges can show greater care for their students if they recognize and attend to the costs students and their families bear as students build new informational trust networks. At the very least, doing so would require not making light of those costs. College faculty and staff should not, for instance, cavalierly challenge students to outgrow or move beyond or rebel against the worldviews and habits of those with whom they grew up even when doing so would improve their trust networks. Faculty should also be careful not to impose those costs for their own partisan or sectarian purposes. A college education should have the potential to be transformative without being an exercise in conversion. Setting out to convert students to a particular position, value system, cause, or concern exploits the opportunity a student's trust provides, and may impose costs on them to benefit an end they may not value. It thus betrays their trust.

Note that teachers can make this mistake in nonpolitical ways, merely by falling back on their habits as researchers when they enter the classroom. A scholarly career will be filled with the development of compelling arguments for precise conclusions, of figuring out not only how and what to think about a particular question, but also ways to convince others to think that way. An undergraduate course that shows care for the costs its students might bear shouldn't operate in exactly the same way. Teaching students how to think like historians or chemists or accountants should not be an exercise in converting them to the worldviews of the majority of historians or chemists or accountants.

Colleges can also care for students as they refurbish and revise the students' informational trust networks by working to equip them with the tools to handle these changes and the effects these changes may have on the students' social ties. Coming to inhabit a new trust network can place strains on students' social ties if it becomes increasingly hard for them to speak with people who trust sources they no longer do, and who do not trust the sources they are coming to trust. This difficulty is magnified if they also stop sharing a sense of the appropriate criteria to use when judging trustworthiness. If we want to help students lessen those strains, we need to teach them not only how to inhabit a possibly new informational trust network, but also how to find ways of continuing to engage with people who occupy the trust networks they have left behind.

Trust networks shape which sources of information we rely on directly. So, one could shift from one network to another by relying on different sets of sources as one thought through a problem or argued for the aptness of a suggestion or solution. There isn't anything particularly unsavory or disingenuous about thinking under various constraints, even if those are constraints we would reject or resist in other circumstances. We do that all the time. Sitting on a jury, we reason about the facts of the case in accordance with the rules of evidence, accepting only those sources that have proper evidentiary authority under the law. When we watch a play or movie or read a novel, we suspend certain forms of disbelief and think about the action of the story within the constraints of its genre or imagined world. Similarly, we can adopt the constraints imposed by a particular informational trust network in thinking with one group of people and a different set of constraints when thinking with another group without in any way dividing our self, our allegiances, or our values.

Back home in her rural community, a student might discuss her parents' plans for their farm without bringing to bear the scientific methods she has learned as an agronomy major or relying on the USDA recommendations she has learned to interpret and give credence to in her classes. She doesn't have to scoff at these sources the way her father does, but she can still choose not to depend on them for the points she wants to make. In talking to her parents, she relies on the same sources they do, which she would never think of citing in her agronomy paper, and she ignores the sources they distrust even if she would happily rely on them when discussing the same issue with her classmates or making her own plans. If she has come to conclude that some of the sources her parents rely on aren't trustworthy, she can avoid them or raise concerns about them that are internal to her parent's trust networks, without thereby abandoning her commitments or acting inauthentically.

How well such a strategy can work may depend on how distinct and distant the informational trust networks her parents occupy are from the one she has built in college. Imagine that her aim is not merely to get through conversations with her parents without a fight, but to bring her experience, wisdom, and judgment to those discussions with the hopes of thereby improving the plans they make. If the trust network she has learned to inhabit at college is wholly distinct from that of her parents, then the only way for her to engage in this conversation with her parents will be to abandon all she has learned at college, and to accept as sound judgments that rely on information sources she no longer trusts. That would make it impossible for her to bring what she has learned and finds valuable to the discussion even if she could manage to take up their trust network in order to talk more easily with them.

One advantage of teaching students to inhabit an open-minded trust network rather than a broadly scientific one is that it is less likely to be completely distinct from the networks students inhabit at the beginning of college. If the student has learned the skills of flexible and charitable thinking and intellectual humility, she is in a better position to weave together and engage with both the networks her parents inhabit and the broadly scientific one they distrust. She will be able to see more clearly the value of the sources they rely on and the sorts of challenges they might raise to a more scientific approach, while also being able to see how various scientific sources might contribute to her parents' deliberations. Beyond helping them to build open-minded trust networks, colleges can help their students manage the shift from one trust network to a new one both by giving them this framing and by teaching them more explicitly how to make the sorts of moves across trust networks gestured at above. Imagine, for instance, that the agronomy student mentioned above is aware of not only the power and reach of various scientific results concerning the effects of various farming techniques on crop yields, but also where such general methods can overlook the particular variances that occur from place to place or crop to crop. Imagine that she has been taught not only these general principles, but also how to engage with criticisms of each perspective from the other, and taught by people who are open to the potential value local knowledge like hers can bring to the questions they ask and the problems they try to solve. She would be better equipped to bring new information and knowledge to her parents' conversation in ways that are internal to that conversation, even if they also broaden it. She would not be left to merely assert the superiority of her college-produced expertise and information or defend it from within its own perspective. To the extent that college equips her with these tools and thus enables her to maintain her ability to have such conversations with her parents or her home community, it helps her manage the social costs her education might otherwise have imposed on her. By giving her these tools, her teachers would show care for her as well as for those who have entrusted them with her education.

Finally, teachers can show care for their students and the communities that sent them by showing appreciation for those communities' worth and values. This doesn't require treating them as customers who are always right or showing complete deference to their points of view and pledging not to have any effect on students' trust networks. Rather, it requires something like a manifest attentiveness to students' value, their existing social ties, and the shared values that may help fortify those ties. One way to show such attentiveness is to make classrooms safe spaces for experiencing the transformative effects involved in building new informational trust networks. To reiterate a point from chapter 5, safe spaces are not meant to prevent students from encountering challenge; rather, their purpose is to ensure that the process of being vulnerable to being changed does not also harbor dangers, whether of failure, ridicule, or condemnation. Different kinds of classroom environments can fail to be safe for this kind of work. In some, students face derision and ridicule from teachers or their fellow students for expressing the perspectives they bring from home. Students from religious backgrounds or who grew up poor or not knowing anyone with a college degree may find it hard to ask questions or raise points that stem from their experiences or perspective if these are far from the views expressed comfortably by most of their peers. They may have the sense that raising such issues is somehow out of bounds or will mark them as hopelessly foreign or backward. In other classrooms, students may face derision and ridicule for experimenting with giving up one outlook for new ways of thinking about the world, or for entertaining ideas and positions others reject. Such derision is as likely to come from their peers as from their teachers, and it is as likely to occur outside of class as in. The general presumptions that can make a student feel unsafe to bring some of her own background and beliefs into an academic setting extend well beyond the sorts of controversial social issues that make the news.

Consider students in a science class who come to college inhabiting a locally grounded or religiously based trust network, try to bring up an observation or challenge that stems from those networks, and are dismissed for being unscientific. Think, for instance, of Robin

Wall Kimmerer's first encounter with her advisor at forestry school, which I quoted in chapter 1. She told him she wanted to study botany to learn why asters and goldenrod looked so beautiful together. His dismissive response—"I must tell you that *that* is not science. That is not at all the sort of thing with which botanists concern themselves"— let her know that this wasn't a space that might value or take seriously potential insights she brought from home.[3]

Teachers can work to make their classrooms safe environments for intellectual experimentation and play, and for trying out new ideas, perspectives, and habits of thought by explicitly describing them that way and modeling such behavior. They can be encouraging when students make mistakes or try on a view before deciding it doesn't or shouldn't fit. They can remind students that insofar as classrooms are playgrounds, some of what happens there should stay there, and everyone in class should refrain from passing judgment on what students say as they are working things out. At the same time, they can remind students that for such spaces of intellectual experimentation to work, everyone has to be mindful of everyone else, and aware that in stretching out their minds they aren't hitting each other in the face. One strategy for doing this is to point out to students at the beginning of the semester the range of people, outlooks, and backgrounds among their classmates, and to remind them that all of them have a right to be there and have something to contribute, and that the rest of them will play a role in whether that happens. In doing so, it is important to explicitly highlight a wide range of relevant circumstances and positions and to make visible those that are likely to be overlooked or invisible on your campus. Having taught at a large urban minority-serving and rather diverse university for many years, the version I recently gave my own students looks like this:

Assume that the following people are in this class:

A member of the military
A Republican
Someone with severe anxiety or depression
Someone with a very sick relative
Someone with care responsibilities for a young sibling or their own
children

Someone who has survived sexual assault or other trauma

An undocumented immigrant

Someone who is gay or lesbian or bisexual or queer or loves someone who is

Someone who is trans or gender non-conforming or loves someone
who is

A feminist

A Black Lives Matter activist

Someone with undiagnosed ADHD or dyslexia or on the autism
spectrum

Someone who is very religious (though not necessarily Christian)

Someone who is isolated and lonely

Someone who has no private quiet space of their own

Someone who doesn't speak English at home

Someone who was home-schooled

Someone who has been or is related to someone incarcerated

Someone who is or is related to a police officer

Someone who grew up in a small town

Someone who has never been to a small town

Someone who has a long commute

Someone who lives on or near campus

Someone experiencing food or housing insecurity

They are all welcome here and have as much right to learn in an environment where they feel they belong as you do.

Whether they get it depends on what the rest of us do.

Please make the effort to help each other learn.

The aim of such a handout, as with all the messages and actions in
this section, is to show care for students in ways that honor their trust.

9. Trust the Students

Students place their informational trust networks in the hands of
teachers and colleges and allow them to act in ways that change
those networks. That is not a passive process: teachers are not trust
surgeons, shaping trust networks while their students sleep. But even

if they are active participants in the transformation college helps them make, students only change and learn if they accept the possibility that what happens in class might change them in these deep and intimate ways. To be and to be seen as trustworthy stewards of this process, colleges need to do more than be competent at the task entrusted to them. Colleges also need to manifest responsiveness to their students' vulnerability and dependence, especially when these arise because of the students' trust. One way for teachers to manifest that responsiveness is to take seriously the challenges and criticisms students raise to the work being done and its value. By doing so, teachers not only demonstrate their trustworthiness but also model inhabiting an open-minded trust network, one that values remaining open to challenge and criticism. Note, however, that teachers who take students' challenges seriously and are open to the possibility that their own thinking requires change are also vulnerable to those students: to being potentially changed by what they say. The thought of being vulnerable to being changed by what students say can provoke anxiety in teachers, which can in turn generate a kind of protective arrogance and unthinking confidence in their own ideas and methods. Teachers can overcome such anxiety while remaining open in this way if they learn to trust their students as their students trust them.

Trusting students need not involve being converted by them. It does, however, require that a teacher remains open to the possibility that what students say can change how he thinks, both about his students and about the world. It requires that he is willing to learn from his students even as he teaches them. (It also requires that students be trustworthy in their turn.)

Teachers who think of the informational trust network they inhabit and try to help their students inhabit as open-minded will find it easier to learn from their students. Since such a trust network does not draw boundaries that allow its inhabitants to merely dismiss certain sources of information or lines of thought, teachers do not assert their expertise within it by dismissing challenges. They demonstrate expertise and trustworthiness by genuinely engaging with challenges and then being open to learning from them. This openness is easier if teachers genuinely value the kinds of expertise their students bring into their classes, recognizing it as more than merely a lesser form of the teacher's own expertise. Teachers who do this often frame the work of their classes differently—not as the laying down of a set of expert-approved ideas, techniques, and bits of information, but as joint explorations of questions or issues for which the skills the class aims to teach will be useful. If teachers take up such joint projects with their students, they can more easily place themselves in a reciprocally trusting relationship. One way to do this is to work together on projects or problems for which the teacher does not already know the answer, or for which students' prior knowledge and experience can be a resource. In such projects, the teacher is not so much the final authority as a knowledgeable guide and resource. It is much easier to demonstrate trustworthiness via reciprocal trust in such work.

10. Reach Out Beyond the Campus

So far, the suggestions canvassed here concern what happens in and on college campuses. But ultimately, one point of all this work is to help address and reduce the anxiety some parents and communities feel in sending their children off to college. To address that anxiety, colleges need not only to be trustworthy, but to give students and their parents and communities the opportunity to see that they are, and why. They need to give them a better sense of what happens at college and why they can feel safe in trusting the college to do what it does. If a college does in fact deserve a community's trust, then it needs to make that case to them, hear what drives their anxiety, and try to respond to it. Even in the era of helicopter parenting and easy forms of communication, what happens on a college campus is often opaque to those outside it, especially if they have not themselves spent time on a campus. Even when students continue to live at home, what they study is more and more likely to be beyond the reach of their parents, and so it can be hard for parents to understand what is going on in those classrooms. Everyone who can read learned to read, and even if they have no idea what goes into the teaching of reading, they can watch as their child develops (or fails to develop) reading skills. But unless a parent works in finance or management or as a biologist, she is unlikely to know enough about finance, management, or biology to follow the development of her child who is majoring in these fields. She is thus unable to competently judge whether her child is getting a good education or whether that education is indoctrinating him in some way she would object to if she understood. For students who come from families and communities where no one or almost no one has a college education, this distance is even more pronounced. Moreover, much of the transformative effects of college happen outside the classroom, in interaction with peers and with activities that are not always familiar to parents and communities back home. For parents who did not attend college, or who did not attend a college like the one their child is attending, this aspect of college can seem even more opaque. Ironically, many of the parents who are most likely to have good reasons to be distrustful are the ones who do the least oversight and know the least about what their students are doing. Helicopter parenting is a practice of the well-off and college-educated.[4]

Colleges can work to calm the anxiety that arises from these forms of opacity by consciously reaching out to parents and communities to make more visible what they do. There are several models for this. Community engagement partnerships between a college or university and the communities that surround it, and community-engaged research projects that involve college researchers working alongside community members to solve community problems or address community needs, can build ties between people working in colleges and people living and working in various communities. They can provide windows from those communities into some of what happens in colleges or how college professors think and act. They can also open windows into communities so that those who work and teach on campus and did not grow up in such communities can better understand what happens there and the informational and social trust networks they inhabit. Many of these efforts involve those who work or study in a college or university reaching out to the communities that surround them, so there is some danger that this outreach will all be done on the college's terms and through its own lens regarding what matters and is of value. Genuinely participatory community engagement and community-centered outreach are difficult to undertake, and require time, care, and a great deal of humility on the part of those from university settings. They often require work to overcome past interactions that were neither reciprocal nor community-focused and the reasonable suspicions these have generated.

If the aim is to give students, parents, and communities reason to trust the educational process that happens in colleges and universities, then there may also need to be forms of outreach that involve inviting those from outside to campus. Here are two ideas for what that might look like. A college or university might offer its expertise to surrounding (and perhaps even distant) communities as an aid to helping them with the problems they identify and wish to solve, serving as something like a beefed-up research library for community organizations. An office of community engagement could act as a kind of switchboard, fielding outside requests for help and connecting them with relevant faculty. This would require compiling and maintaining lists of willing, trained faculty and their relevant areas of expertise, and perhaps keeping tabs on the partnerships that grow out of these queries to make sure they serve to build trusting relationships. Faculty who wish to devote some of their time and energy to such an effort could be trained in the methods and practices of engaged research, and could apprise the central office of their willingness and range of expertise. Colleges could incentivize this by considering such work in promotion, tenure, and pay decisions. The aim would be to invite communities to see and treat nearby colleges and universities as potential partners and resources, rather than as foreign or hostile presences.[5]

Second, individual instructors or departments might invite their students' parents or family members to brief informational sessions about their class or program. Many K-12 schools arrange an evening early in the school year where parents are invited to come to the school to meet their children's teachers in a kind of simulated school day. Teachers invite parents into their classrooms and give them a sense of what their class is like, what it teaches, and what they expect from their students. They answer questions, and, if all goes well, show themselves to be trustworthy. Even this brief encounter can make it easier for parents to ask questions later or reach out to a teacher if their child encounters difficulties during the school year. In the context of higher education, this would, of course, require modification. Students are adults in their own right and so are protected by privacy rights. Since college instructors generally have no way of contacting parents directly, this kind of invitation would have to run through students, allowing students who wished to keep their parents from knowing about their studies or lives to do so. In addition, many students study in colleges far from where their parents live (even when they commute from home), so these kinds of events would have to be virtual, which presents its own kind of challenges. It might be that the best an instructor could do would be to create a short recording or video or document designed for students to share with family members. In the current political climate, instructors in some places might be rightly concerned about their words being taken out of context or used to target them. But however an instructor worked out the logistics, the mere process of imagining one's students' family members and what she might say to them about what she was trying to do for her students would, I suggest, be helpful in thinking about her own trustworthiness. I opened this book describing an encounter I had many years ago with a student and his father. One of the things that made that encounter so surprising at the time was that I had never really considered how my teaching might be regarded by my students' parents, and what, if anything, I might owe them in terms of consideration or concern as I worked to educate their children. Perhaps if I had thought about engaging in the sort of outreach suggested here, I would have been moved to get clearer, for myself and for my students, about what I was trying to do and whether they had reason to trust me to do it. Engaging in this kind of outreach might also help colleges and their faculty members to see if and where they are less trustworthy than they think.

11. Consider Diversity of Background in Hiring

Another way to bring community members onto campus is to employ them. College staff and faculty who have principal responsibility for overseeing and carrying out the education of students are themselves college educated. They thus inhabit the sorts of trust networks college graduates inhabit. They also, by and large, found that network and the process of learning to inhabit it sufficiently rewarding and exciting that they wish to pass it on to others. In addition, a very high percentage of college faculty grew up in households where the adults had a college education and in communities where having a college education was the norm.[6] This demographic imbalance can create blind spots as colleges set policy and structure their activities, and it can also help to create and maintain norms that make it hard for those few faculty without such a background to feel comfortable bringing up such issues in formal and informal conversations with their colleagues. As a result, colleges can be insufficiently aware of and attentive to the sorts of social and economic costs they impose on their students and their students' families and communities.

Colleges are less likely to overlook those costs if, among their faculty, staff, and administration, there are enough people who come from the sorts of backgrounds where those social costs are most likely to be felt. This suggests that colleges have a reason to attend to the background of those they hire, and to work to make sure there is diversity in background amongst them. The diversity required here is about neither viewpoint nor identity (which is not to take a stand on whether these forms of diversity also have value). Diversity of background concerns where people are from and the attendant social costs of their own college education. Faculty or staff who grew up in a socially conservative rural community or who were the first in their family to go to college are more likely to recognize the social costs a college education might impose on students from a similar background. They are more likely to recognize ways education puts stress on social ties, or why certain students perceive the college environment as unwelcoming or hostile. They may also have better ideas about what would help. This can be true even if they no longer share the views of their family and community or look like the students who face similar challenges where they work. A professor who grew up in a religious Christian household but who drifted away from his faith in college or afterward might nevertheless be more attentive to the costs faced by his college's religious Muslim students than a faculty member who grew up in a secular environment and faced no issues with his faith in college. An advisor who grew up in rural poverty will be more aware of the ways financial precarity shapes a college experience and the policies that can ease that, even if the poor students on her campus all come out of urban environments and she now lives a solidly middle-class adult life. Beyond merely diversifying faculty and staff this way, colleges need to make this diversity apparent to students, their families, and others on campus. Unlike diversity of identity or viewpoint, diversity of background can go unnoticed if not welcomed and highlighted. In discussions of curricula, teaching practices, and student life policies, it is important that the college hear and seriously consider the observations and insights of people from diverse backgrounds. The point here is not to absolve those whose upbringing meant that college imposed no strains on their social relationships from concern with these issues, nor to task those who are more aware of these issues with doing all the work to solve them. Nor is it to force into the public space of the college all the details of everyone's background. But very often those backgrounds are seen as something to be hidden or overcome, so those who have such backgrounds are often uneasy about making them known. Colleges would do well to work to recognize the value those from diverse backgrounds bring to their campuses, increase their number, and support those who want to bring that value into policy, curricular, and pedagogical discussions.

Conclusion: Why This Matters Beyond the College Campus

The suggestions canvassed in chapters 5 and 6 point to the kinds of curricular, pedagogical, and institutional changes colleges and universities might undertake in order to earn and receive the trust of their students and their students' families and communities. These changes would help lower the social costs some students currently pay to get a college education. That might make higher education a less tempting wedge issue for politicians. And even if it didn't, it would make those institutions better at their primary mission of improving students' capacities for thought and knowledge. There is, however, a third kind of reason for pursuing some or all of the suggestions outlined here.

Democracy is a way of living together in which people work out together how to live together.[7] When groups of citizens are inscrutable to one another, when they have real trouble understanding where their fellow citizens are coming from or the sense of their positions or concerns, they cannot do this work together. Moreover, it is all too easy in such circumstances for citizens to impute bad motives to each other or treat their fellow citizens as if they don't know their own minds or interests. That, of course, just drives them further apart, as such attitudes are generally (and often rightly) read as showing disdain and contempt for those who are not understood. The politics of resentment easily finds its fuel.

When different groups of people in a society inhabit non-overlapping informational trust networks, such mutual inscrutability is often the result. When two groups of people see wholly separate sources of information as trustworthy and distrust the sources the other group relies on, then they cannot easily converse or work anything out together, even if they should somehow come to want to do so. A society might reach this point or somewhere close to it through any number of processes: those that produce social isolation or involve the marginalization of some by others, or those that generate a fractured media and social landscape or drive increasing polarization. But however a society winds up there, when its social landscape isolates people on distinct cognitive islands, it faces a genuine democratic crisis. Such a landscape portends disaster for a society trying to sustain its democratic character.

One common response to the recognition of this phenomenon is to call for more or better education, and in particular, better civic education. If only everyone could be taught the rules of civil discourse or toleration or the value of free speech, then they could all start to work together again. But it should now be clear that whether this is an appropriate response depends on the kind of education imagined. If educational institutions try to bolster democracy by engineering their students' informational trust networks in ways that line them all up with those of college-educated elites, or with a broadly scientific outlook that tends to overlook and dismiss the lived experience of those who have been overlooked and harmed by social institutions, then it will not bridge our divides. Those who defend such educational practices often think of themselves as living on something like the cognitive mainland, and understand their task as reaching out to what they perceive as the cognitive islands in their society and transporting the children they find there onto the supposed mainland. It should be no surprise that such a process sows distrust and resentment and does very little to actually stitch together the cognitive landscape of the society. It is, after all, the perception that institutions of higher education are doing just that which is generating the sorts of anxieties I have been concerned to understand and respond to.

If, however, educational institutions helped their students build and inhabit informational trust networks based in open-mindedness, and did so in ways that fostered and deserved trust, then they, and their students, could play a different social role. Students who learned to be open-minded in the sense laid out in chapter 5 would inhabit an informational trust network that contains regions that overlap with the trust networks of those on various cognitive islands. This would put them in a good position to learn the further skills needed to serve as bridges between them. Teachers whose work in educational institutions did not isolate them, and who learned from and trusted their students, could also serve as bridges in the same way. On such a model, it would be the work of education not to bolster the defenses of its territory but to stitch together the cognitive fabric of the whole society. By teaching in this way and building this kind of informational trust network, institutions of higher education would make themselves into hubs of interaction across cognitive divides: places where conversation across those divisions is fostered and nurtured. In doing so, colleges and universities could become trustworthy models of genuinely open democratic conversation. Rather than serving as political fodder for those seeking wedge issues to exploit, colleges and universities could be beacons of democratic interaction. They could become places where our mutual vulnerability before one another is met not with anxiety, but with trust. To build such trust, however, colleges and universities will need to be more open. They will need not only to be, but to be subject to, the change they want to see in the world. I hope to have provided some conceptual tools with which to begin.

Acknowledgments

The story of this book has many beginnings. About fifteen years ago, Harry Brighouse began recruiting me into the philosophy of education the way someone might recruit another person into a left-wing political organization or an intelligence service: an invitation here, some funding there, an exciting opportunity, a chance to meet some new and interesting people, and before long I was hooked. About ten years ago, Harry and Mike McPherson asked me to help start what became the Center for Ethics and Education. The Spencer Foundation generously funded it, and working on its projects has been one of the best and most fulfilling parts of my career. The Center's fingerprints are all over this book.

In the spring of 2020, like everyone else, we found ourselves forced to make up ways to take things online. We had been planning to welcome a new cohort of our Summer Graduate Institute to a two-week in-person session that summer. Instead, we organized a set of day-long Zoom sessions, and, like so many others, we tried to make it seem exciting by taking the opportunity to invite outside speakers to discuss their work with our students. We hosted a session with Gina Schouten to discuss a draft of a paper of hers that offered a response to conservative charges about left-wing professors indoctrinating their students with left-wing ideals.[1] At the time I was also preparing to teach a graduate seminar on trust and had just read C. Thi Nguyen's paper "Trust as an Unquestioning Attitude." It struck me that Nguyen's account of trust shed light on the issue Schouten was addressing, and the spark that led to this book flashed into being. What started as an email to Harry, then Gina, in the summer of 2020 turned into a short paper and then a podcast, and then three articles and several talks, and now, here we are.

If you are lucky as a philosopher, then occasionally a good idea will just pop into your head. If you are very lucky, then you will have people around you to nudge that idea forward and give it the attention and engagement necessary to develop it from an email-sized thought into something more substantial. I am a very lucky philosopher. Harry routinely suggested moving this to the next level ("Why don't you write a short piece?" "Why don't we do a podcast episode?" "Why don't you turn those pieces into a short book?"). Gina, Mike, Paula McAvoy, Carrie Welsh, Jennifer Morton, Sarah Stitzlein, Anne Eaton, Annette Martín, Bailey Szustak, and Jamie Hamilton all read some or other early version of the initial idea and provided useful guidance and encouragement. Carrie produced the episode of the Ethics and Education podcast called "Teaching, Indoctrination and Trust" in the spring of 2021, which wound up being the first public appearance of these ideas. Audiences at meetings of the North American Association for the Philosophy of Education and the American Philosophical Association Central Division, as well as the Graduate Student Conference on the Philosophy of Education at CUNY, raised helpful questions about the material on the social costs of education. Steven Cahn, Doug Yacek, and Randall Curren offered invitations to publish articles on this topic in anthologies they were assembling, which gave me a chance to work out more of the details during 2021 and 2022. The results: "The Social Costs of a College Education" appeared in *Academic Ethics Today*, edited by Steven Cahn (Lanham, MD: Rowman and Littlefield, 2022); "Education, Trust and the Conversation of Democracy" appeared in *The Cambridge Handbook of Democratic Education*, edited by Julian Culp, Johannes Drerup, and Douglas Yacek (Cambridge: Cambridge University Press, 2023); and "College Teaching, Indoctrination, and Trust" appeared in the *Handbook of Philosophy of Education*, edited by Randall Curren (New York: Routledge, 2023). I am grateful to all of them for their feedback and for the opportunities they provided for building up the account and trying out its parts.

In the final stage of actually writing this book, I have been lucky once again to find so many careful and thoughtful readers: Elizabeth Branch Dyson at the University of Chicago Press has not only stewarded this project through the approval process but given me both sage advice about how to write what I hope is a generally accessible book and detailed editorial feedback on several drafts. The two anonymous reviewers she lined up offered many helpful suggestions and criticisms, and the process of responding to those has helped me make the book better. The members of the 2022–23 Center for Ethics and Education Graduate Summer Institute read and discussed the "Social Costs" paper with me in the summer of 2022, and then we workshopped a draft of the whole manuscript for a day and a half in the summer of 2023. Jamie Herman also read and commented on subsequent revisions. My friend Michael Friedman, neither a philosopher nor an education researcher, gave me extensive and helpful comments on a very late draft on a remarkably tight deadline. The production team at Chicago, including Elizabeth Ellingboe and Evan Young, caught my misplaced commas and infelicitous phrasings and turned a string of words into this book. Many parts of the book are better thanks to all their care and attention, and I am grateful for all of it. The many flaws that no doubt remain are my own damn fault.

Ideas don't get to grow, and books don't get to be written, without financial support that gives authors time to think and write. I am grateful to the University of Illinois at Chicago for a sabbatical leave in the spring of 2021 and another research leave in the spring of 2023 that made it possible for me to write this book. In fact, I owe many debts of gratitude to UIC: to my colleagues in the philosophy department for providing such a supportive, stimulating, and enjoyable place to work for the past twenty-seven years; to my students, who have put up with me as I (slowly and imperfectly) learned to teach them, and from whom I have come to understand the variety of paths people take to and through college; and to all the others who make it possible for a chronically underfunded urban public minority-serving research university to continue to strive not only to push the boundaries of knowledge but to provide our students the quality of education they deserve.

Nothing I have done that is worth doing over the past thirty-two years is not the better for Caroline Guindon's support, love, and deep intelligence and wisdom. I have been made a better teacher, better writer, and better person trying to live up to her example and her loving vision.

When college does not go well for students and imposes the sorts of costs I discuss in this book, faculty, staff, and administrators rarely see the full effects. A student stops coming to class or turning in assignments. Perhaps they come to ask for help once or twice, perhaps not. Maybe they fail a class or end up with a low grade. Maybe they leave college altogether. Whatever is going on in their lives outside of class and college is mostly invisible to us. And then they are gone. It is parents and communities who see the full effects and try to pick up the pieces. While the ideas at the center of this book popped into my head as a teacher and philosopher, the book itself only took shape because of my experience as a parent. I am oh so grateful to all three of my children—Jacob, Raphaël, and Clara—for the joy and laughter and love they have brought to my life, but I would not have been able to write this book without the many lessons I have learned from Clara. This one's for you.

Notes

Chapter One

1. See chapter 5 for an extended discussion of charitable thinking and its value.
2. J. Causey, S. Lee, M. Ryu, A. Scheetz, and D. Shapiro, *Completing College: National and State Report with Longitudinal Data Dashboard on Six- and Eight-Year Completion Rates*, Signature Report 21 (Herndon, VA: National Student Clearinghouse Research Center, November 2022). The cohort that started college in 2010 had a 54.1 percent graduation rate, so things are improving. Graduation rates are much higher for four-year nonprofit colleges (private 77.8 percent, public 68 percent) than for for-profit (47.6 percent) and public two-year schools (43.1 percent), but that still leaves more than a fifth of students in private nonprofit colleges failing to graduate.
3. Todd, quoted in Jennifer Morton, *Moving Up without Losing Your Way: The Ethical Costs of Upward Mobility* (Princeton, NJ: Princeton University Press, 2019), 29.
4. Robin Kimmerer, *Braiding Sweetgrass: Indigenous Wisdom, Scientific Knowledge and the Teachings of Plants* (Minneapolis, MN: Milkweed Editions, 2013), 33–34.

Chapter Two

1. For some vivid examples of parents trusting colleges when they shouldn't, see Laura T. Hamilton, *Parenting to a Degree* (Chicago: University of Chicago Press, 2016).
2. For some of the important social implications of our necessary reliance on expertise, see C. Thi Nguyen, "Transparency Is Surveillance," *Philosophy and Phenomenological Research* 105, no. 2 (2022): 331–61.
3. C. Thi Nguyen, "Trust as an Unquestioning Attitude," *Oxford Studies in Epistemology* 7 (2023): 214–44.

4. Nguyen, "Trust," 232.
5. Nguyen, "Trust," 225.
6. Nguyen, "Transparency Is Surveillance"; Elijah Millgram, *The Great Endarkenment: Philosophy for an Age of Hyperspecialization* (Oxford: Oxford University Press, 2015).
7. This description of the "reading wars" is indebted to the reporting of Emily Hanford. See, for instance, Emily Hanford, "Sold a Story: How Teaching Kids to Read Went So Wrong," podcast, APM Reports, American Public Media, last accessed January 30, 2024, https://features.apmreports.org/sold-a-story/.
8. Tamar Schapiro, "Compliance, Complicity and the Nature of Non-Ideal Conditions," *Journal of Philosophy* 100, no. 7 (2003): 329–55.
9. Bo Rothstein, *Social Traps and the Problem of Trust* (Cambridge: Cambridge University Press, 2005).
10. Anthony Bryk and Barbara Schneider, *Trust in Schools: A Core Resource for Improvement* (New York: Russell Sage Foundation, 2002).
11. Bryk and Schneider, *Trust in Schools*, 20.
12. Bryk and Schneider, 22–26.
13. For some examples of what these failures can look like, see Anthony Abraham Jack, *The Privileged Poor: How Elite Colleges Are Failing Disadvantaged Students* (Cambridge, MA: Harvard University Press, 2019).
14. See, for instance, Annette Baier, "Trust and Antitrust," *Ethics* 96, no. 2 (1986): 231–60; Karen Jones, "Trust as an Affective Attitude," *Ethics* 107, no. 1 (October 1996): 4–25.
15. Stanley Fish, *Save the World on Your Own Time* (New York: Oxford University Press, 2008).

Chapter Three

1. The image of pipes and filters comes from C. Thi Nguyen, "Trust as an Unquestioning Attitude," *Oxford Studies in Epistemology* 7 (2023): 214–44.
2. For one example of how such policies play out, see Elizabeth A. Armstrong and Laura T. Hamilton, *Paying for the Party* (Cambridge, MA: Harvard University Press, 2013).
3. For a compelling instance of this process, see Eli Saslow, *Rising Out of Hatred: The Awakening of a Former White Nationalist* (New York: Anchor, 2019). Thanks to Randall Curren for suggesting its relevance.
4. David Baker, *The Schooled Society: The Educational Transformation of Global Culture* (Palo Alto, CA: Stanford University Press, 2014). Baker describes a shift in university education from a system modeled on imitating classical forms to one based on the sorts of scientific thinking being emphasized here.
5. Baker, *The Schooled Society*.
6. Though I've given examples from fields in the arts and sciences, a similar case could be made for this point in pre-professional education. It is, after all, the idea that there is general knowledge about business management, physical

therapy, or teaching, for instance, that justifies there being programs of study in colleges devoted to these occupations.

7. This is how I recall Sheryl Underwood describing the benefit of a liberal arts education during a speech at the commencement ceremonies of the College of Liberal Arts and Sciences at the University of Illinois at Chicago, May 7, 2017. I do not know of a published or otherwise accessible version of this speech.

8. For some discussion of the ways colleges do this independent of what they teach, see Paul Tough, *The Inequality Machine: How Universities Are Creating a More Unequal World—and What to Do about It* (New York: Random House, 2021); Sandy Baum and Michael McPherson, *Can College Level the Playing Field? Higher Education in an Unequal Society* (Princeton, NJ: Princeton University Press, 2022).

Chapter Four

1. For examples of these features of elite campus culture, see Anthony Abraham Jack, *The Privileged Poor: How Elite Colleges Are Failing Disadvantaged Students* (Cambridge, MA: Harvard University Press, 2019); Paul Tough, *The Inequality Machine: How Universities Are Creating a More Unequal World—and What to Do about It* (New York: Random House, 2021); Elizabeth A. Armstrong and Laura T. Hamilton, *Paying for the Party* (Cambridge, MA: Harvard University Press, 2013); Patrick J. Carr and Maria J. Kefalas, *Hollowing Out the Middle: The Rural Brain Drain and What It Means for America* (Boston: Beacon Press, 2009).

2. On the hidden costs of college, see Nancy Kendall et al., *The True Costs of College* (London: Palgrave Macmillan, 2020); Armstrong and Hamilton, *Paying for the Party*; Jack, *The Privileged Poor*.

3. Ethical costs are measured in what Morton calls "ethical goods": goods tied to what we value most in life that are particular and not easily replaced. Her main examples are close ties to particular people like family, friends, and neighbors. Jennifer Morton, *Moving Up without Losing Your Way: The Ethical Costs of Upward Mobility* (Princeton, NJ: Princeton University Press, 2019). The works cited above also discuss such costs, although without using Morton's terminology.

4. Morton, *Moving Up without Losing Your Way*, 29.

5. Jack describes a program at the university he studies which provides free tickets for campus cultural events for poorer students but distributes them in a different line than the one where students line up to pay for their tickets (Jack, *The Privileged Poor*, 190). Students who wanted the subsidized tickets thus had to out themselves as poor. In contrast, Swarthmore College has a cash-free campus—everything available on campus, from the coffee sold at the coffee cart in the library to the tickets for cultural events, is freely available to students who show an ID. Nothing distinguishes those who pay a fee as part of their tuition for these items from those who have that fee covered as part of their financial aid.

6. Tara Westover, *Educated: A Memoir* (New York: Random House, 2018), 228.

7. This section draws on descriptions of rural communities in Arlie Hochschild, *Strangers in Their Own Land: Anger and Mourning on the American Right* (New York: New Press, 2016); Robert Wuthnow, *The Left Behind: Decline and Rage in Rural America* (Princeton, NJ: Princeton University Press, 2018); Jennifer Sherman and Rayna Sage, "Sending Off All Your Good Treasures: Rural Schools, Brain-Drain, and Community Survival in the Wake of Economic Collapse," *Journal of Research in Rural Education* 26 (2011); Carr and Kefalas, *Hollowing Out the Middle*.

8. This is one of the themes of Carr and Kefalas, *Hollowing out the Middle*.

9. On the devastating economic effects of borrowing money to start but not finish college, see Peter Cappelli, *Will College Pay Off? A Guide to the Most Important Financial Decision You'll Ever Make* (New York: PublicAffairs, 2015); William G. Bowen and Michael McPherson, *Lesson Plan* (Princeton, NJ: Princeton University Press, 2016).

10. Morton, *Moving Up without Losing Your Way*; Carr and Kefalas, *Hollowing Out the Middle*.

11. James C. Scott, *Seeing Like a State: How Certain Schemes to Improve the Human Condition Have Failed* (New Haven, CT: Yale University Press, 1998).

12. Scott, *Seeing Like a State*, 11–22.

Chapter Five

1. I take this term and its description, as well as the category of echo chambers, from C. Thi Nguyen, "Echo Chambers and Epistemic Bubbles," *Episteme* 17, no. 2 (2020): 141–61.

2. Sandy Baum and Michael McPherson, *Can College Level the Playing Field? Higher Education in an Unequal Society* (Princeton, NJ: Princeton University Press, 2022).

3. This need not make the choices they make biased. Some news outlets' strategy for attracting attention is to sustain a well-deserved reputation for thorough and objective reporting. Nevertheless, those whose economic model relies on advertising are basically in the business of capturing attention for their advertisers and sponsors. For a particularly stark version of this dynamic, see the reports on Fox News's coverage of the aftermath of the 2020 US presidential election, which shows that the network chose to promote what it took to be false and unsubstantiated claims of electoral fraud to avoid losing viewers. For a general overview of these reports, see "Dominion Voting Systems v. Fox News Network," Wikipedia, last updated July 25, 2023, 14:39, https://en.wikipedia.org/wiki/Dominion_Voting_Systems_v._Fox_News_Network.

4. Nguyen, "Echo Chambers and Epistemic Bubbles"; Kathleen Hall Jamieson and Joseph N. Cappella, *Echo Chamber: Rush Limbaugh and the Conservative Media Establishment* (Oxford: Oxford University Press, 2008).

5. For one particularly in-depth discussion of this sort of process, see Eli Saslow,

Rising Out of Hatred: The Awakening of a Former White Nationalist (New York: Anchor, 2019).

6. For instance, there is a rich and growing literature in philosophy and other fields about various forms of social ignorance that block members of privileged or dominant groups from developing access to usable knowledge about the injustice of the conditions that sustain their position. See, for instance, Shannon Sullivan and Nancy Tuana, *Race and Epistemologies of Ignorance* (Albany: SUNY Press, 2007).

7. Both are taken by Enlightenment thinkers and their intellectual descendants as hallmarks of the use of reason to understand and engage with the world, and for this reason they are often conflated. For a helpful discussion of the difference, and its origins in Enlightenment thought, see Samuel Fleischacker, *What Is Enlightenment?* (New York: Routledge, 2013). For discussion of the difference between reasoning guided by norms of rationality and reasoning guided by norms of openness to challenge, see Anthony S. Laden, *Reasoning: A Social Picture* (Oxford: Oxford University Press, 2012).

8. Note that this may not thereby reduce all the social costs she faces in going to college. She may still have to devote time to her studies and shirk duties of care at home. She may still have to move away from home after college to find a job that interests her and exercises her newly acquired abilities, or that pays enough to cover the financial costs of college. She may still find the social atmosphere at her chosen college to be alienating, hostile, or merely deeply unfamiliar.

9. This notion of charity is common in philosophy. It is to be distinguished from merely being nice or lowering standards to help someone clear a bar.

10. Kyla Ebels-Duggan, "Autonomy as an Intellectual Virtue," in *The Aims of Higher Education: Problems of Morality and Justice*, ed. Harry Brighouse and Michael McPherson (Chicago: University of Chicago Press, 2015), 82.

11. For an example of such cases and methods of pedagogy in the field of educational ethics, see Meira Levinson and Jacob Fay, *Dilemmas of Educational Ethics: Cases and Commentaries* (Cambridge, MA: Harvard Education Press, 2016).

12. On the difficulty of making expertise transparent to non-experts, see C. Thi Nguyen, "Transparency Is Surveillance," *Philosophy and Phenomenological Research* 105, no. 2 (2022): 331–61.

13. The question of disclosure is a central one in the teaching of controversial social issues. For a discussion of the reasons for and against disclosing in those contexts, see Diana E. Hess and Paula McAvoy, *The Political Classroom: Evidence and Ethics in Democratic Education* (New York: Routledge, 2014), 182–203.

Chapter Six

1. Collin O'Neil, "Lying, Trust, and Gratitude," *Philosophy & Public Affairs* 40, no. 4 (2012): 301–33. O'Neil argues that we owe gratitude to those who trust us,

but that the gratitude in question is not like that for a gift, but like that for an honor.

2. For ease of reference and discussion, I continue the numbering of the suggestions from chapter 5.

3. Robin Kimmerer, *Braiding Sweetgrass: Indigenous Wisdom, Scientific Knowledge and the Teachings of Plants* (Minneapolis, MN: Milkweed Editions, 2013), 33–34.

4. Laura T. Hamilton, *Parenting to a Degree* (Chicago: University of Chicago Press, 2016).

5. For one example of what this kind of work might look like, see Seth Moglen, "Sharing Knowledge, Practicing Democracy," in *Education, Justice, and Democracy*, ed. Danielle Allen and Rob Reich (Chicago: University of Chicago Press, 2013), 267–84.

6. According to a 2022 study published in *Nature: Human Behaviour*, only 28.7 percent of professors did not have a parent with a college degree, and only 19.2 percent had no parent with any experience in college. Allison C. Morgan et al., "Socioeconomic Roots of Academic Faculty," *Nature Human Behaviour* (2022): 1–9.

7. I fill out and defend this description of democracy and tie it to open-mindedness in "How Democracy Doesn't End," in *Democratic Multiplicity*, ed. James Tully et al. (Cambridge: Cambridge University Press, 2022), 25–39.

Acknowledgments

1. The paper was eventually published as Gina Schouten, "The Case for Egalitarian Consciousness Raising in Higher Education," *Philosophical Studies* 179, no. 9 (2022): 2921–44. At the time it had the less professionally buttoned-down title "Should We Be the College Teachers Our Uncles Warned Us About?"

Bibliography

Armstrong, Elizabeth A., and Laura T. Hamilton. *Paying for the Party*. Cambridge, MA: Harvard University Press, 2013.

Baier, Annette. "Trust and Antitrust." *Ethics* 96, no. 2 (1986): 231–60.

Baker, David. *The Schooled Society: The Educational Transformation of Global Culture*. Palo Alto, CA: Stanford University Press, 2014.

Baum, Sandy, and Michael McPherson. *Can College Level the Playing Field? Higher Education in an Unequal Society*. Princeton, NJ: Princeton University Press, 2022.

Bowen, William G., and Michael McPherson. *Lesson Plan*. Princeton, NJ: Princeton University Press, 2016.

Bryk, Anthony, and Barbara Schneider. *Trust in Schools: A Core Resource for Improvement*. New York: Russell Sage Foundation, 2002.

Cappelli, Peter. *Will College Pay Off? A Guide to the Most Important Financial Decision You'll Ever Make*. New York: PublicAffairs, 2015.

Carr, Patrick J., and Maria J. Kefalas. *Hollowing Out the Middle: The Rural Brain Drain and What It Means for America*. Boston: Beacon Press, 2009.

Causey, J., S. Lee, M. Ryu, A. Scheetz, and D. Shapiro. *Completing College: National and State Report with Longitudinal Data Dashboard on Six- and Eight-Year Completion Rates*. Signature Report 21. Herndon, VA: National Student Clearinghouse Research Center, November 2022.

Ebels-Duggan, Kyla. "Autonomy as Intellectual Virtue." In *the Aims of Higher Education: Problems of Morality and Justice*, edited by Harry Brighouse and Michael McPherson, 74–90. Chicago: University of Chicago Press, 2015.

Fish, Stanley. *Save the World on Your Own Time*. New York: Oxford University Press, 2008.

Fleischacker, Samuel. *What Is Enlightenment?* New York: Routledge, 2013.

Hamilton, Laura T. *Parenting to a Degree*. Chicago: University of Chicago Press, 2016.

Hanford, Emily. "Sold a Story: How Teaching Kids to Read Went So Wrong." Podcast. APM Reports, American Public Media. Accessed January 30, 2024. https://features.apmreports.org/sold-a-story/.

Hess, Diana E., and Paula McAvoy. *The Political Classroom: Evidence and Ethics in Democratic Education*. New York: Routledge, 2014.

Hochschild, Arlie. *Strangers in Their Own Land: Anger and Mourning on the American Right*. New York: New Press, 2016.

Jack, Anthony Abraham. *The Privileged Poor: How Elite Colleges Are Failing Disadvantaged Students*. Cambridge, MA: Harvard University Press, 2019.

Jamieson, Kathleen Hall, and Joseph N. Cappella. *Echo Chamber: Rush Limbaugh and the Conservative Media Establishment*. Oxford: Oxford University Press, 2008.

Jones, Karen. "Trust as an Affective Attitude." *Ethics* 107, no. 1 (October 1996): 4–25.

Kendall, Nancy, Denise Goerisch, Esther C. Kim, Franklin Vernon, and Matthew Wolfgram. *The True Costs of College*. London: Palgrave Macmillan, 2020.

Kimmerer, Robin. *Braiding Sweetgrass: Indigenous Wisdom, Scientific Knowledge and the Teachings of Plants*. Minneapolis, MN: Milkweed Editions, 2013.

Laden, Anthony S. "How Democracy Doesn't End." In *Democratic Multiplicity: Perceiving, Enacting and Integrating Democratic Diversity*, edited by James Tully et al., 25–39. Cambridge: Cambridge University Press, 2022.

———. *Reasoning: A Social Picture*. Oxford: Oxford University Press, 2012.

Levinson, Meira, and Jacob Fay. *Dilemmas of Educational Ethics: Cases and Commentaries*. Cambridge, MA: Harvard Education Press, 2016.

Millgram, Elijah. *The Great Endarkenment: Philosophy for an Age of Hyperspecialization*. Oxford: Oxford University Press, 2015.

Moglen, Seth. "Sharing Knowledge, Practicing Democracy." In *Education, Justice, and Democracy*, edited by Danielle Allen and Rob Reich, 267–84. Chicago: University of Chicago Press, 2013.

Morgan, Allison C., Nicholas LaBerge, Daniel B. Larremore, Mirta Galesic, Jennie E. Brand, and Aaron Clauset. "Socioeconomic Roots of Academic Faculty." *Nature Human Behaviour* 6 (2022): 1625–33.

Morton, Jennifer. *Moving Up without Losing Your Way: The Ethical Costs of Upward Mobility*. Princeton, NJ: Princeton University Press, 2019.

Nguyen, C. Thi. "Echo Chambers and Epistemic Bubbles." *Episteme* 17, no. 2 (2020): 141–61.

———. "Transparency Is Surveillance." *Philosophy and Phenomenological Research* 105, no. 2 (2022): 331–61.

———. "Trust as an Unquestioning Attitude." *Oxford Studies in Epistemology* 7 (2023): 214–44.

O'Neil, Collin. "Lying, Trust, and Gratitude." *Philosophy & Public Affairs* 40, no. 4 (2012): 301–33.

Rothstein, Bo. *Social Traps and the Problem of Trust*. Cambridge: Cambridge University Press, 2005.

Saslow, Eli. *Rising Out of Hatred: The Awakening of a Former White Nationalist*. New York: Anchor, 2019.

Schapiro, Tamar. "Compliance, Complicity and the Nature of Non-Ideal Conditions." *Journal of Philosophy* 100, no. 7 (2003): 329–55.

Schouten, Gina. "The Case for Egalitarian Consciousness Raising in Higher Education." *Philosophical Studies* 179, no. 9 (2022): 2921–44.

Scott, James C. *Seeing Like a State: How Certain Schemes to Improve the Human Condition Have Failed*. New Haven, CT: Yale University Press, 1998.

Sherman, Jennifer, and Rayna Sage. "Sending Off All Your Good Treasures: Rural Schools, Brain-Drain, and Community Survival in the Wake of Economic Collapse." *Journal of Research in Rural Education* 26 (2011).

Sullivan, Shannon, and Nancy Tuana. *Race and Epistemologies of Ignorance*. Albany, NY: SUNY Press, 2007.

Tough, Paul. *The Inequality Machine: How Universities Are Creating a More Unequal World—and What to Do about It*. New York: Random House, 2021.

Westover, Tara. *Educated: A Memoir*. New York: Random House, 2018.

Wuthnow, Robert. *The Left Behind: Decline and Rage in Rural America*. Princeton, NJ: Princeton University Press, 2018.

Index

higher education: critics of, 8–9, 31,
66–68, 119; diversity of institutions
of, 8, 86; focus on, 7–8; harms of,
9–10; informational trust networks
and, 24, 35–45. *See also* college

Hochschild, Arlie, 130n7

home, difficulty of returning after
college, 4, 56, 62, 64

humanities classes, 48, 96–99

humility, 86, 93–95, 97, 109; needed for
community outreach, 115; shown
in gratitude, 104

inclusion, 6, 43, 66, 71

indoctrination, 1, 6, 24, 31–32, 66, 71, 115

inequality, 50–51, 79

information: generic vs. situated,
21–22, 47; limitations on access to,
75–82; role of in thinking, 3, 14, 16;
sources of, 34, 46

informational ideology, 21–25, 34–35;
and broadly scientific sources,
45–50; and local knowledge,
59–61; and moral righteousness,
61–62; shared within disciplines
and professions, 39; and solidarity,
62–64

informational trust networks, 3, 15–25,
34; vs. beliefs and values, 45;
broadly scientific, 6, 45–51, 58–59,
66–71, 85–86; and challenges, 82;
and cognitive islands, 5, 120–21;
among college graduates, 58–59;
college's shaping of, 24, 29, 32–33,
36–45, 56–57, 112–14; dangers of,
20; evaluation of sources within,
93; in marginalized communities,
62–64; mixed, 65; moving between,
90, 107–9; open-minded, 82–86,
109–10; in religious households,
61–62; in rural communities,
59–61; and social ties, 4, 23–24,
41–45; specialized in research,
106; as tools for understanding, 4;

trustworthiness of, 21; value of for
knowing, 73–75

informational valleys, 75–77

inscrutability: of those with distinct
trust networks, 5, 23, 64–65; as
threat to democracy, 119–20

intellectual humility. *See* humility

interdisciplinary collaboration, 39–40

introductory classes, 91

Jack, Anthony Abraham, 128n13,
129nn1–2, 129n5

Jamieson, Kathleen Hall, 130n4

Jones, Karen, 128n14

Kefalas, Maria, 129n1, 130nn7–8,
130n10

Kendall, Nancy, 129n2

Kimmerer, Robin Wall, 9–10, 111

knowing: being better at, as aim of
college education, 21, 49, 67–69,
73–75, 82–85; improved by open-
mindedness, 84

knowledge: general vs. local, 21–22,
46–48, 59–64, 85, 109; and trust
networks, 18–24, 45

Laden, Anthony, 131n7, 132n7

learning: as collaborative, 28–29; via
interaction with peers in college,
42–45; role of trust in, 28, 33; from
students, 113; and vulnerability,
12–14

legibility: via education, 36–39;
importance of, for action, 69–70;
mutual, among college graduates,
59; value of scientific thinking in
producing, 49, 68, 70

Levinson, Meira, 131n11

locally situated knowledge, 21–22,
59–61, 69

marginalized communities, 57, 62–64

McAvoy, Paula, 131n13